Dedicated to
Those from America
Who Fought Bravely in the Anti-Fascist War in China

献给
在世界反法西斯战争中国战场上
英勇战斗的美国人

Compiled by

the Information Office of Yunnan Provincial People's Government

the Information Office of Zhejiang Provincial People's Government

Yunnan Daily Press Group

Zhejiang Provincial Archives

编者

云南省人民政府新闻办公室

浙江省人民政府新闻办公室

云南日报报业集团

浙江省档案馆

The Memory of History
历史的记忆

Masterminded by

the State Council Information Office of the People's Republic of China

策划

中华人民共和国国务院新闻办公室

Published by China Intercontinental Press

五洲传播出版社

The Memory of History

历史的记忆

The Hump

驼峰航线

Route

Opening the Hump Route

开辟"驼峰航线"

On December 7, 1941, the Japanese launched a sudden attack on Pearl Harbor and the Pacific War broke out.

1941 年 12 月 7 日，日本偷袭珍珠港，太平洋战争爆发。

In May 1942, the Japanese occupied Burma and invaded the west of China's Yunnan Province and cut the land transportation link along the Burma Road,which was called the "last Chinese transfusion line". China and the United States had to open the Hump Route jointly.

1942 年 5 月，日军占领缅甸并侵入中国云南西部，被称为"中国最后一条陆路输血线"的战略运输线滇缅公路被切断。中美被迫共同开辟"驼峰航线"。

Flights over The Hump involved flights at high altitude over difficult terrain and bad weather conditions unparalleled in the history of world civil and military aviation.

"驼峰航线"是世界航空史和军事史上飞行高度高、气候条件恶劣、最为艰险的空中战略运输线。

❶ The Himalayas 喜马拉雅山脉　　　❷ Hengduan mountains 横断山脉

❸ Dinjan 汀江　　❹ Myitkyina 密支那　　❺ Baoshan 保山　　❻ Chuxiong 楚雄　　❼ Kunming 昆明　　❽ Yunlong 云龙　　❾ Putao 葡萄

❿ Sadiya 萨地亚　　⓫ Lijiang 丽江　　⓬ Xichang 西昌　　⓭ Yibin 宜宾　　⓮ Luzhou 泸州　　⓯ Chongqing 重庆　　⓰ Chengdu 成都

⓱ Bhamo 八莫　　⓲ Lashio 腊戍

- - - - - - - The Hump Route
驼峰航线

Burma Road (959.4 kilometers long)
滇缅公路 (长 959.4 公里)

The Hump Route was very dangerous. With mountain peaks over 17,000 feet, the planes had to reach the height of 25,000 feet.
"驼峰航线"非常艰险,山峰高度超过 1.7 万英尺,飞行高度最高达 2.5 万英尺。

Bad weather conditions were often featured by strong airflow,low air pressure, hailstones and frosts. Flying this route, the accident rate was extremely high.
恶劣的气候以及强气流、低气压和经常发生的冰雹、霜冻,使飞机在飞行中随时都有坠毁和撞山的危险,飞机失事率高得惊人。

The veteran pilot said that, on clear days, they could fly along the route by the reflection from the remains of crashed planes. The valley covered with broken pieces of those aircraft hence had a cold metallic name "the Aluminum Valley".

"驼峰航线"的老飞行员说：在天气晴朗时，我们完全可以沿着战友坠机碎片的反光飞行。他们给这条撒落着战友飞机残骸的山谷取了个金属般冰冷的名字——"铝谷"。

Building the Airports
修建机场

In China's Yunnan Province,a dozen airports for large aircraft were built in Kunming, Chengkung, Luliang, Chanyi, Yanggai, Yunnanyi, Baoshan and other places.
在中国云南修建了昆明、呈贡、陆良、沾益、羊街、云南驿、保山等 10 多个可供大型飞机起降的机场。

Without heavy mechanical equipment, the construction was completed all by manual labor. Pulling stone rollers weighting 3-5 tons, the workers were singing to the rhythm of their work songs and moving slowing...

修建机场没有重型机械设备，完全靠大量的人力投入。劳工们拉着3至5吨重的石碾子，唱着歌，踩着号子的节奏，缓缓地前行着……

While the airports were still under construction, planes were already flying the Hump Route in the shadow of war.
驼峰机场正在抢修，飞机已经在战争乌云密布的"驼峰航线"上飞行。

The Hump Aircraft Types
驼峰机型

From May 1942 to August 1945,more than 100 planes took off and landed each day among the air freighters.The fighter planes and bombers were in charge of convoy and combat missions in the China-Burma-India War Theater.During the three years and three months, China and the U.S. used a total of some 2,000 air freighters,fighter planes and bombers in the combat.

自 1942 年 5 月至 1945 年 8 月,各型运输机平均每天有 100 多架次的起降。战斗机和轰炸机主要承担着护航和中缅印战区的作战任务。在 3 年零 3 个月的时间里,中美双方共投入各种运输机、战斗机和轰炸机约 2000 架。

The units who participated in the Hump Flights were the American Ferry Command (before Dec. 1, 1942), the Army Transport Command (after Dec.1, 1942) and the China National Aviation Corporation(CNAC). The units who defended the Hump Flights were the 10th and 14th Air Force.

在"驼峰航线"担任空运任务的是美国空运队（1942年12月1日之前）、美国陆军运输队（1942年12月1日之后）和中国航空公司；保卫"驼峰航线"的有美国陆军第10航空队、第14航空队。

Air Freighters 运输机

The main units involved in the Hump Flights were the Army Transport Command (ATC) and the China National Aviation Corporation (CNAC).

CNAC put 10 planes into the air transport in 1942 and 20 in 1943, and the number rose to 30 in 1944.

ATC put 25 planes into the air transport in 1942, and the number gradually rose thereafter.

The China-India ATC (founded in December 1942) possessed 629 air freighters of different types till 1945. The main types among these were C-46 and C-47 with a rough total of 600.

All the air freighters flying over the Hump were the best transport planes at that time. The C-53, C-54, C-46, C-47 and DC-3 were made by the Douglas Company of America. The DC-3, C-53 and C-47 had almost the same size and structure, and the DC-3 was a passenger plane.

参加驼峰空运的主要单位是美国陆军运输队和中国航空公司。

中国航空公司 1942 年投入空运的飞机是 10 架、1943 年是 20 架,1944 年增加至 30 架。

美国陆军运输队 1942 年投入空运的飞机为 25 架,随后逐步增加。

到 1945 年美国陆军运输队印中联队(成立于 1942 年 12 月)有各型运输机 629 架,主力机型为 C-46、C-47,大约有 600 架左右。

参加驼峰空运的飞机在当时来说,都是比较好的运输机。C-53、C-54、C-46、C-47、DC-3 型飞机均为美国道格拉斯公司制造。DC-3、C-53、C-47 型飞机的尺寸和结构基本相同,DC-3 为客机型。

The C-53 and C-47 were cargo aircraft with 28.9 m wingspan and 19.63 m fuselage. They carried two piston engines that developed 1,200 horsepower. Their largest take-off weight was 127, 000 kg, the maximum commercial carrying capacity was 3,100 kg, the best cruising speed was 274 km per hour, and the best cruising altitude was 6,000 m – 7,000 m. The DC-3 passenger plane could hold 21 – 28 passengers.

C-53、C-47 为货运型，其翼展均为 28.9 米，机身长 19.63 米，装两台活塞式发动机，每台功率 1200 马力，最大起飞重量 12700 公斤，最大商务载重量 3100 公斤，巡航速度 274 公里／小时，最大飞行高度 6000-7000 米。DC-3 客机型可乘客 21-28 人。

The C-46 airplane was a little better than the C-53, C-47 and DC-3. It had 2 engines that developed 2,000 horsepower with 32.92 m wingspan and 23.27 m fuselage.Its largest take-off weight was 25, 400 kg, the maximum commercial carrying capacity was 3, 640 kg or 40 armed soldiers, the best cruising speed was 301 km per hour, and the maximum air-range was 1, 883 km.

C-46 型飞机的性能比 C-53、C-47 和 DC-3 略好些，也装两台发动机，但功率较大，每台功率为 2000 马力，翼展为 32.92 米，机身长 23.27 米，最大起飞重量 25400 公斤，商务载重量 3640 公斤或载 40 名全副武装士兵，巡航速度 301 公里／小时，航程可达 1883 公里。

The C-54 air freighters for military use were the best. It was a long-distance cargo plane with 4 piston engines that developed 1,450 horsepower per engine. Its wingspan was 35.81 m and the fuselage was 28.6 m. Its largest take-off weight was 33,113 kg, the maximum commercial carrying capacity was 9,980 kg, the best cruising speed was 365 km per hour, and the air-range might reach 4,025 km.

C-54 型军用运输机的性能最好，为远程货运飞机，装有 4 台活塞式发动机，每台功率为 1450 马力，翼展 35.81 米，机身长 28.6 米，飞机起飞重量 33113 公斤，商务载重量 9980 公斤，巡航速度 365 公里／小时，航程达 4025 公里。

Fighter Planes 战斗机

Defending the Hump Flights were the 10th and 14th Air Forces, whose fighter planes mainly included the P-38, P-40, P-47, P-51 and P-61.

保卫驼峰空运的主要是第 10 航空队、第 14 航空队等,战斗机主要有 P-38、P-40、P-47、P-51、P-61 等。

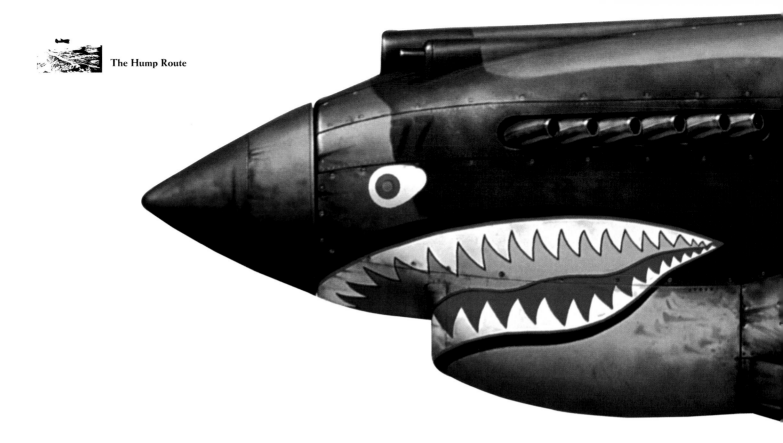

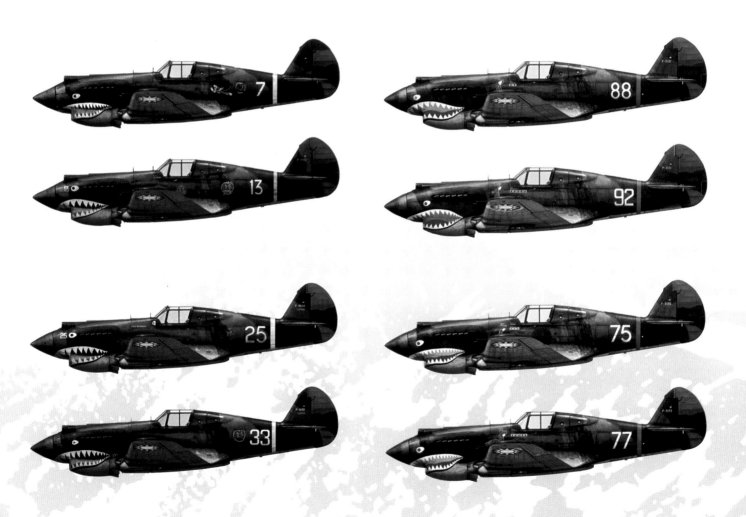

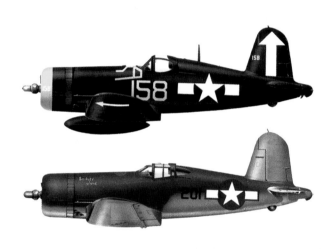

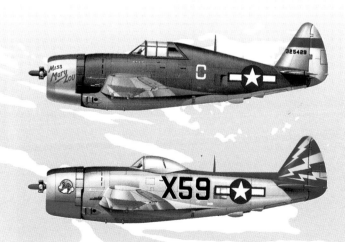

Bombers 轰炸机

Types of bombers mainly included the B-24, B-25 and B-29.
轰炸机主要有 B-24、B-25、B-29 等。

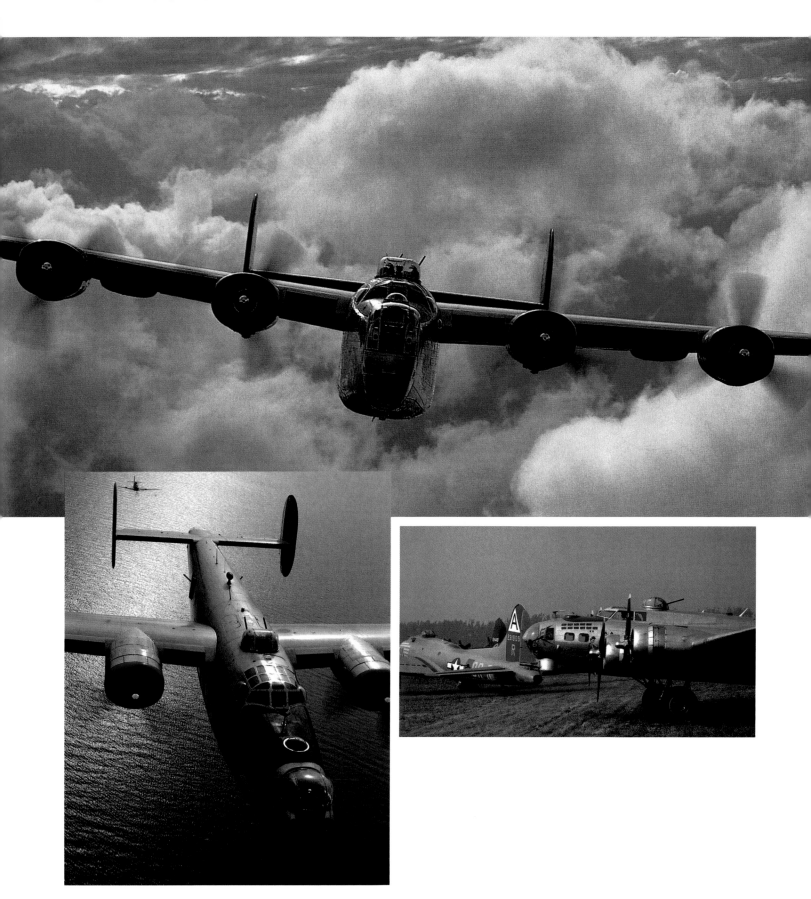

Transportation Hardships

艰难的运输

It took 2 months to transport war materials from the United States to Karachi, a distance of 12,000 miles. Then, another month was needed to rail transport them to Dinjan in India's Assam State.

战略物资用 2 个月的时间从美国运到卡拉奇，路程 1.2 万英里。之后，再用 1 个多月的时间通过铁路运抵印度阿萨姆邦的汀江。

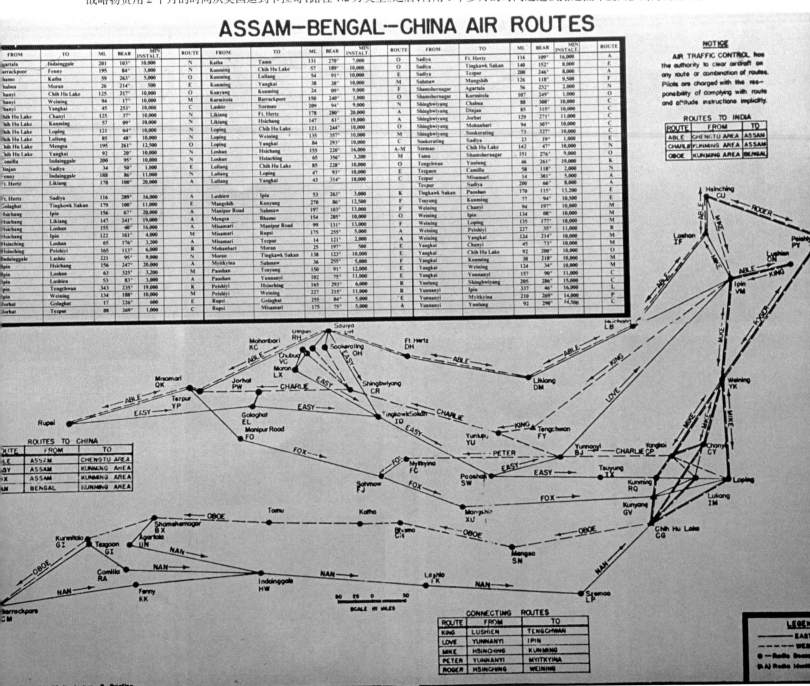

War materials were transported to China's Kunming through the Hump Route. The trucks, horse wagons or even rickshaws took them to the battlefield. In the period of over 3 years, the Hump Flights transported more than 800,000 tons of war supplies to China. On average, there were over 100 air freighters flying over the Hump daily.

这些战略物资通过"驼峰航线"运到中国昆明，再用汽车甚至马车、人力车转运到战争前线。在 3 年多的时间里，"驼峰航线"共向中国运输战略物资 80 多万吨，平均每天有 100 多架运输机在航线上穿梭飞行。

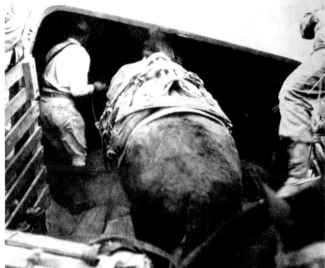

The Hump was known as the Death Route. In three years and three months, China and the United States lost 609 planes and 1500 pilots. James Dalby, a pilot of CNAC, kept a track record of the CNAC's 62 air freighters from 1943. By August 1945, 44 aircraft had either crashed or gone missing.

"驼峰航线"又称"死亡航线"。在 3 年零 3 个月的时间里，中美共坠毁和失踪飞机 609 架，牺牲和失踪 1500 多名飞行员。中国航空公司飞行员詹姆斯·达尔比从 1943 年开始对 62 架中国航空公司的运输机飞行状况进行追踪记录，至 1945 年 8 月，其中 44 架运输机失事和失踪。

Fella —

I have Reported your Position — Sorry about the Rations that I dropped My crew did Not obey orders And dropped them Too Soon —

Help will be on its way Soon — IF you can walk toward the Wreck There is a Large House Just below it

This is my Log Book for the day I sighted Steve Fiduk. Notice I was flying #94. This airplane crashed near Kunming killing the crew. The airplane was piloted by Capt. "Ridge" Hammel. This was the second accident for Hammel. In 1943 he was co-pilot on an airplane piloted by Joe Rosbert (ex AVG). They slammed into a snow covered mountain on the first ridge at about 16,000 feet. Though badly injured Rosbert and Hammel survived a many week trek out. The Chinese Radio Operator was killed on impact. (Courtesy of James Dalby)

The C-47 of CNAC piloted by Don Kord made a forced landing in the paddy fields near Dinjan in India in a storm. The crew survived and walked back to their base.

唐·科德驾驶的中航 C-47 运输机在暴风雨中迫降在印度汀江附近的稻田里，机组人员幸免于难，只能步行返回基地。

An air freighter crashed when hit by strong airflow and all the crewmembers died.

A C-46 hit the top of the Western Hills by Lake Dianchi due to instrument failure.

Another C-46 crashed because of engine failure.

A C-54 number 272403 crashed near the Shaba Base in India.

A C-109 air freighter crashed after running out of fuel.

A C-47 number 73 hit cliffs on the western bank of the Lake Dianchi when preparing to land at Kunming's Wujiaba Airport.

...

一架运输机因遇到强气流而撞山爆炸,机组成员全部遇难。

一架 C-46 飞机因仪器故障撞上了滇池湖的西山顶。

一架 C-46 飞机因引擎失灵而坠毁。

一架 C-54 飞机(编号 272403)坠毁在印度沙巴基地附近。

一架 C-109 运输机因燃料耗尽而坠毁。

一架 C-47 运输机(编号 73)准备在昆明巫家坝机场降落时,撞毁在滇池西岸巨大的山崖上。

......

Searching for Aircraft No. 53
寻找53号坠机

On June 3, 1996, a local hunter discovered a crashed aircraft on the Pianma Saddle of Gaoligong Mountain in Yunnan,China.

1996 年 6 月 3 日，一名猎人在中国云南高黎贡山片马垭口发现一架坠机。

The local Chinese government immediately sent out a team to investigate and record the findings, and organized the local people to keep a 24-hour watch over the aircraft.

消息传来,中国当地政府立即派员前往坠机现场进行勘察记录,并组织数批百姓日夜守护着坠机……

After having identified and measured the aircraft's size, code number and orientation of crash, it had been confirmed that the aircraft was the CNAC's No. 53 aerotransport that crashed more than 50 years ago.

经过对飞机机型、编号、坠落方位等辨认和测量,确认这就是 50 多年前坠毁的中国航空公司 53 号运输机。

On March 11, 1943, the Hump pilot James R. Fox and two Chinese pilots Tan Xuan (Thom) and Wang Guoliang (Wong), piloting CNAC's aircraft No. 53 aerotransport, left Wujiaba airport in Kunming for Dinjan, India. While flying over Gaoligong Mountain in Yunnan, China, the plane lost contact with the ground.

1943 年 3 月 11 日，驼峰飞行员詹姆斯·R·福克斯与中国飞行员谭宣、王国梁驾驶着中国航空公司 53 号运输机，从昆明巫家坝机场起飞，飞往印度汀江。在飞越中国云南高黎贡山时 53 号机与地面

Accident Report for the C-53 No. 53 Aircraft
C-53型53号机失事报告

11 March 1943   C-53 #53   DINJAN   DEAD: 3
CREW: Pilot: J. R. Fox
C/P: Thom (Chinese)
R/O: Wong (Chinese)

This CNAC aircraft departed Kunming, China enroute to Dinjan, India. It crashed in the daytime, while flying the passes, under an overcast sky. Apparently it got into a downdraft and crashed in the jungle 50 feet from the top of a mountain, on the east side.It is about 3 miles south of the Hpimaw-Lokou road. This territory was enemy occupied at the time of the crash.The fate of the crew is now known, all aboard were killed. (25° 54' — 98° 41')

The friends of James R. Fox found that aircraft No.53 had crashed into a valley, while flying across Gaoligong Mountain.
詹姆斯·R·福克斯的战友们在执行任务经过高黎贡山时，发现 53 号机坠毁在一个山洼里……

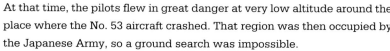

At that time, the pilots flew in great danger at very low altitude around the place where the No. 53 aircraft crashed. That region was then occupied by the Japanese Army, so a ground search was impossible.

战友们冒着生命危险，绕着 53 号机坠毁地点作超低空飞行。然而，这一地区被日军占领，地面搜寻无法实现。

After aircraft No.53 had been lost for three months, another Hump pilot came to Kunming,China.He was Fletcher Hanks.He was deeply impressed by James' story which was widely spread in the army.He thought it was a soldier's duty to find his comrade-in-arms, so to find James became his mission.

在 53 号机失事 3 个月后，另一位驼峰飞行员来到中国昆明，他就是弗莱彻·汉克斯。詹姆斯·R·福克斯的故事在军营中广泛流传，给弗莱彻·汉克斯留下了深刻印象。他觉得寻找战友同样是军人的职责，他在心中暗暗把寻找詹姆斯·R·福克斯当成了自己的使命。

An old Chinese man who knew well Gaoligong Mountain told Hanks: Because the mountain was enshrouded in virgin forest and the elevation was over 6,000 meters, even the local folks would not risk going into the place. On October 21, 1944, the news of the recovery of Gaoligong Mountain from the Japanese army came to Hanks. He was overjoyed, and asked for permission to search for aircraft No. 53. When his request was approved, he and two others, Hurmose and Kansk, joined the "searching team".

熟悉高黎贡山的中国老人告诉弗莱彻·汉克斯，这座山海拔6000多米，是原始森林，当地人都不敢贸然进山……1944年10月21日，收复高黎贡山的消息传来，弗莱彻·汉克斯欣喜若狂，申请寻找53号坠机。在得到批准后，弗莱彻·汉克斯和另外两个战友赫尔莫斯、康斯克一起加入了"搜索队"。

When entering the mountain, beasts, bramble, oxygen depletion, disease and starvation threatened the team like a devil.Having walked in the forests for 9 days and nights, half of the team members fell ill. Things became even worse when they ran short of food. So Hanks reluctantly decided to go back.

"搜索队"进入高黎贡山后，野兽、荆棘、缺氧、疾病和饥饿恶魔般地缠住了他们。在9天9夜的跋涉中，"搜索队"大半病倒，并且食物短缺，弗莱彻·汉克斯等人被迫抱憾而归。

After he returned to Kunming, Hanks compared the coordinates of their return trip with those of the No.53 aircraft, and found that the point from where they turned back was less than 1 mile from the site of the crashed aircraft.

回到昆明的弗莱彻·汉克斯，把返程座标和53号坠机座标对照，遗憾地发现"搜索队"原来距坠机不到1英里……

Across the ocean in America, James' mother uttered these words when she was dying: "Little James will come home from the distant east!" Fox's niece Pamela J. Smith believed that her uncle, whom she never got chance to see, was already dead.But she yearned to fulfill her grandma's wish to bring her uncle home and bury him beside her grandma.Pamela visited many veteran Hump pilots to collect more information about her uncle so as to pinpoint the site of the crashed No.53 aircraft.

在大洋彼岸的美国,詹姆斯·R·福克斯的母亲在弥留之际,依然念叨:"小吉米会从遥远的东方回家的……"詹姆斯·R·福克斯的侄女帕米拉·J·史密斯相信她从未见过面的叔叔已经不在人世,但她要完成奶奶的愿望,那就是把叔叔接回来,安葬在奶奶的墓旁。帕米拉四处走访驼峰老飞行员,以确认坠机地点。

In America, another "crazy man" who had the strong will to search for the aircraft was F. Hanks. In order to go back to the Gaoligong Mountain one day, the 80-year-old F. Hanks kept exercising himself just as he did in the army. Hearing about Hanks' resolution, some people joked, "You are the Don Quixote who one day will be devoured by vultures on the Himalayas." With boundless pride, Hanks drew himself a cartoon and named it "Mock Myself", under which he wrote, "CNAC NEVER GIVES UP!"

在美国，另一个执着寻找 53 号坠机的"疯子"就是弗莱彻·汉克斯。为了有一天能重返高黎贡山，80 岁的他依然像在军营时一样锻炼着身体。看到弗莱彻·汉克斯寻找 53 号坠机痴心不改，有人开玩笑说："你是一个终有一天要被喜玛拉雅山上的秃鹫吃掉的'唐·吉珂德'。"弗莱彻·汉克斯豪情万丈地画下了这幅"自嘲"漫画，上面写着："永不放弃！"。

In China, another "Don Quixote" was also tirelessly searching for the No.53 aircraft. This man is Mr. Ge Shuya(the right), researcher of the Hump history. Year after year, Ge Shuya spent almost all his time in the Gaoligong Mountain valleys tracking down traces of the crashed aircraft. Having learned about this, Hanks decided to ally himself to Ge Shuya, so as to jointly fulfill the mission.

在中国，另一个"唐·吉珂德"也在不懈地寻找着 53 号坠机，他就是驼峰历史的研究者戈叔亚(右)。他常年奔走在高黎贡山的峡谷中，搜寻着 53 号坠机的踪迹……弗莱彻·汉克斯得知这一消息后，决定与戈叔亚一起来完成共同的愿望。

Two long years have elapsed since the discovery of the No.53 aircraft, during which the Chinese people overcame countless difficulties due to the extreme natural and physiological conditions to faithfully watch over the aircraft. On February 22, 1998, a heavy snowstorm fell on the Gaoligong Mountain. When carrying out his duty, Qu Tiancheng, a 24-year-old young man of the Nu ethnic minority, died right beside the aircraft, holding a bottle of liquor with which he tried in vain to warm himself up. The dust that covered up James, once again blanketed this Chinese youth.

自发现 53 号机残骸后，在长达两年多的时间里，中国百姓一直忠诚地守护着它。1998 年 2 月 22 日，高黎贡山骤降暴雪，24 岁的怒族青年曲天成，揣着一瓶御寒的白酒，倒在了日夜守护的 53 号坠机旁。曾经掩埋过詹姆斯·R·福克斯的尘土再次覆盖在这位中国青年的身上。

Hearing that the aircraft had been discovered, F. Hanks immediately set off for Kunming.
弗莱彻·汉克斯得知发现坠机的消息后,立即飞抵昆明!

Helped by the Chinese soldiers and civilians, the old man completed his 5-day journey to the aircraft-crash site, and stood beside the No.53 aircraft.
在中国军民的帮助下,经过 5 天跋涉,弗莱彻·汉克斯终于站在了 53 号坠机旁。

The old Hump soldier who spent half a century tirelessly searching for the aircraft had eventually made his life-long dream a reality.

这位执着的驼峰老兵见证了半个多世纪的寻找，完成了一生凤愿。

Children of Nujiang Prefecture came to the Pianma Saddle. They wove azalea leaves into the aircraft's shape to pay tribute to the Hump martyrs and cherish the friendship between the Chinese and American peoples. On February 19, 1998, those Nujiang children sent their cloth-scroll painting of their azalea-leaf aircraft to the Aeronautics and Space Museum in San Diego, America. The Museum held a solemn ceremony to accept the precious gift from the distant east.

怒江的小朋友们也来到坠机现场，他们在53号坠机旁用杜鹃树叶摆成了飞机模样，表达中国儿童对驼峰勇士们的深切怀念和对中美两国人民友谊的珍重。1998年2月19日，怒江各民族小朋友做的飞机模型布标，送达美国圣地亚哥航空航天博物馆。博物馆以隆重的仪式接受了这来自东方的珍贵礼物。

In order to better preserve the crashed aircraft that is a valuable witness of the history, on May 27, 1998, the local government carefully moved the aircraft to Pianma Town that is 50 kilometers from the crash site.

为了更好地保护坠机，珍存这一历史见证，1998 年 5 月 27 日，当地政府把 53 号坠机搬运到离坠机地点 50 多公里以外的片马镇。

In Pianma Town, the Chinese army men and civilians held a solemn ceremony to welcome the No.53 aircraft that had woken up from its more than 50-year slumber in the mountain, and to cherish the Hump martyrs who had devoted their lives to peace. 在片马镇，中国军民用隆重的仪式迎接这在深山中沉睡了50多年的53号坠机，缅怀献出生命的驼峰勇士们。

Crashed Aircraft on Mao'er Mountain
猫儿山坠机

On October 2, 1996, two Chinese farmers Pan Qibin (the left) and Jiang Jun (the right), both belonging to the Yao ethnic minority of Guangxi Province, entered a virgin forest on the Mao'er Mountain that was the highest in South China to collect medicinal herbs…

1996 年 10 月 2 日，中国广西瑶族农民潘奇斌（左）、蒋军（右）进入人迹罕至的华南最高峰猫儿山原始森林采药……

They accidentally discovered wreckages of a crashed plane hanging on the cliffs.

……他们在悬崖断壁上发现了飞机残骸。

The local government repeatedly dispatched people to investigate the site, organized the local people to protect the crashed plane and informed the United States about the discovery.

当地政府多次派人到飞机残骸现场勘察，并对现场进行了有效保护，同时把情况通报给美国方面。

The Chinese and U. S. governments spared no efforts to search for remains of the 10 crew members in the virgin forest at an elevation of 2,000 meters.
中美两国人员不遗余力地在海拔 2000 米的原始森林中搜寻 10 名遇难机组人员的遗骸。

The Office of Missing Personnel under the U.S. Department of Defense sent to China an Experts Group headed by Vice Director Allen Leota to join related Chinese departments in the site investigations. It had been confirmed that the plane was the No. 40783 aircraft that crashed 53 years ago. The picture shows the plane's crew.

经美国国防部失踪人员事务办公室副主任艾兰·列奥塔率领的专家小组和中国有关部门实地调查,确认这架飞机就是53年前失事的40783号机。图为美军坠毁飞机机组人员生前合影。

In an accident that occurred on January 14, 1997, an American news reporter who was investigating the site of the crashed plane fell down a 60-meter-deep cliff. With the help of Pan Qibin and the local people, the reporter was rescued successfully.

1997年1月14日,美国记者在飞机残骸现场采访时,不慎摔下60多米深的悬崖。在潘奇斌和当地人民的及时抢救下,这位美国记者成功脱险。

THE WHITE HOUSE

WASHINGTON

March 19, 1997

Pan Qiwen
People's Republic of China

Dear Pan Qiwen:

Thank you very much for your selfless act of heroism in rescuing Voice of America journalist Stephanie Ho after she fell at Maoer Mountain.

Your courageous efforts will be long remembered, not only by Americans and Chinese, but by people across the globe, as an example of compassion that transcends nationalities or cultural differences. You have shown yourself to be a true citizen of the world, and I commend you for your bravery and resourcefulness. On behalf of a grateful nation, please accept my most heartfelt thanks.

Sincerely,

Bill Clinton

Bill Clinton, the President of the United States, wrote to Pan to show his heartfelt gratitude and appreciation in 1997.
1997年，美国总统比尔·克林顿致信潘奇斌，为他救助美国记者的英雄行为表示感谢和敬意。

On January 17, 1997, a ceremony was held at the Capital Airport in Beijing to hand over remains of the crew of the No. 40783 aircraft to the United States.

1997 年 1 月 17 日，在北京首都机场举行了 40783 号机组人员遗骸交接仪式。

Search and Rescue Over the Hump
驼峰救护

During the war-torn years in China, a silk fabric had been sewn on the jacket of each American pilots, on which were Chinese characters that read: "All Chinese Army Men and Civilians Are Requested to Rescue and Protect This Foreign (American) Pilot Who Is Helping China in the Fight".

来华参战的美国飞行员的军装上都缝有这样一块绸布，上面写着"来华助战洋人（美国），军民一体救护"的中文字样。

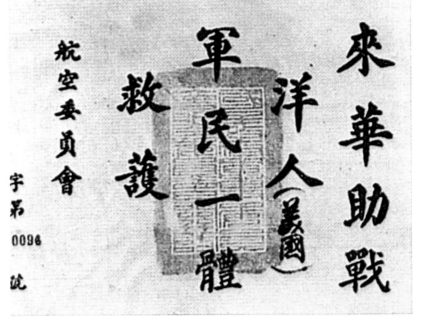

Referred to as the "Xuefu" (blood-written talisman) by the pilots, the little silk fabric had helped rescue many American pilots who got lost amid strange terrain, suffered accidents and forced landings, or baled out after their planes were hit by Japanese gunfire.

这块被飞行员们称为"血幅"的绸布,帮助许多因迷路、事故和被日军击落而迫降、跳伞的美国飞行员得到中国军民的救护。

Roland R. Johnson, a Hump pilot of the Army Transport Command stationed at Baoshan airport, Yunnan, was a joyful, optimistic and affectionate young man. He got along very well with the local farmers. His "pet" in China was an old ox that belonged to one of his farmer friends.

罗兰德·R·约翰逊是驻守在云南保山机场的美国陆军运输队的驼峰飞行员，他乐观豁达，感情丰富。他和当地农民的交情很好，他在中国的"宠物"是一头老牛。

On August 4, 1945, overall victory in China's Anti-Japanese War was drawing closer. With a crew that included the copilot Robert D. Roller and radio operator John T. Carrpil, Captain Roland R. Johnson piloted his C-46 air freighter (code number 107286) to carry out their last mission. Unfortunately, the aircraft crashed at a site some 50 kilometers away from Baoshan airport. It crashed near Shanyang in Yongping, a beautiful and unsophisticated village. Luckily, Captain Johnson and his two men bailed out just before the crash.

1945 年 8 月 4 日，中国抗日战争取得全面胜利在即。机长罗兰德·R·约翰逊与副驾驶员罗伯特·D·鲁勒、报务员约翰·T·卡彼尔驾驶编号为 107286 的 C-46 运输机执行他们最后的空运任务。在离保山机场 50 多公里处，飞机不幸坠毁。坠机地点靠近永平县杉阳——一个美丽古朴的小山村。罗兰德·R·约翰逊和其他两名机组人员在飞机坠毁前跳伞。

Luo Guangpu and other Shanyang farmers saw what happened. Losing no time, they rushed to the site of the accident to search for and rescue the airmen. All the Shanyang farmers coming to the rescue and the three American airmen gave the thumbs up with the words "DINGHAO", which meant "OK" in Chinese. That was their common language to show friendship.

罗光蒲和其他杉阳农民目睹了飞机坠毁全过程。他们急速赶往失事地点搜寻、救护飞行员。前去救助的杉阳农民与3位美国飞行员同时竖起大拇指,用"顶好!顶好!"这一共通的语言传达着友谊。

After the departure of Captain Johnson and his crew from the village, a Shanyang shepherd found a watch that hung on a tree. Later, related American departments confirmed that the watch belonged to John T. Carrpil, the radio operator.

罗兰德·R·约翰逊等机组人员离开杉阳后，一个放羊的杉阳农民在树上拾到了一只手表。经美国有关方面考证，这只手表是报务员约翰·T·卡彼尔的遗失之物。

Although half a century has elapsed, Roland R. Johnson has never forgotten those Shanyang farmers who came to their rescue. He made a model of the C-46 aircraft, and presented it to the Shanyang people as a witness to ever-lasting friendship.

半个多世纪过去了，罗兰德·R·约翰逊从未忘记救助过他们的杉阳人民。他亲手制作了一架 C-46 飞机模型，送给杉阳人民，见证这段长存的友情。

On June 27, 1944, a report reached the Yunnanyi airbase of the American Air Force, saying that Lt. Robert Wesselhoeft had fallen seriously ill while carrying out his duties in Lanping, west Yunnan. Although under the tender care of the Lanping people, Lt. Robert Wesselhoeft needed emergency medical treatment, which was lacking in the small Lanping village.

1944 年 6 月 27 日，美空军云南驿基地接到报告，罗伯特·威瑟尔霍夫特中尉在云南西部兰坪执行任务时身患重病。兰坪民众精心照料罗伯特中尉，但小山村里缺医少药，罗伯特中尉急需救助。

An American plane was dispatched from the Yunnanyi airbase to rescue him, but the 2-day attempt repeatedly failed due to overcast conditions and lack of a landing place. On June 29, Lt. Robert Wesselhoeft's sickness became critical. The American airbase had no choice but to go to Lanping via the precipitous land route. After a hard journey that lasted five long days, the American medical team arrived at Lanping on July 3.

美军营救飞机从云南驿基地前来抢救,但兰坪上空乌云密布,连续 2 天找不到降落地点。6 月 29 日,罗伯特中尉病情恶化。美军基地只得派出医疗队从陆路赶往兰坪,经过 5 天艰苦跋涉,在 7 月 3 日抵达兰坪。

By that time, the lieutenant was breathing with difficulty,and it seemed that he was dying. It was realized that the only hope to save him would be sending him to the war hospital right away.However,it would take more than ten days to reach the American war hospital in India,or at least five days to drive him to the war hospital in Baoshan or Yunanyi. But, he was in critical condition and it seemed unlikely he could stand the ordeal of the trip.The American rescue team was caught in the dilemma.Then the Lanping farmers came up with the suggestion of building a make-do airstrip in the spacious mountain valley for the rescue plane,which the team thought worthy of a try. To build the airstrip meant to race against time, and to win time meant to win Robert's life.The local farmers immediately started the work despite of untold difficulties.

这时,罗伯特中尉呼吸困难,生命垂危,必须及时送往美军战地医院抢救。但是,从兰坪到在印度的美军战地医院有 10 天以上的路程,到保山或云南驿战地医院至少需要 5 天,罗伯特中尉虚弱的身体,已禁不住路途的颠簸和劳累。兰坪农民建议在这空旷的山谷里为营救飞机修建一个临时跑道,美军医疗队认为值得一试。 修建跑道意味着与时间赛跑,赢得时间就赢得了罗伯特中尉的生命。兰坪农民立即在艰难的条件下行动起来。

After strenuous work that lasted 3 days and nights, the farmers had the airstrip completed. Welsh piloted a rescue plane and successfully landed it at Lanping. Lt. Robert Wesselhoeft was eventually saved.

经过 3 昼夜的连续奋战，兰坪农民完成了跑道的修建。威尔士驾驶营救飞机成功降落在兰坪。罗伯特中尉终于得救了。

In the days of the Hump Flights, the local people of Luliang, Yunnan, set up a volunteer wartime rescue team bearing the name "Farmers' Rescue Team". Thanks to the timely help of the Farmer Rescue Team, many wounded pilots were saved on the battlefields. Volunteers of the Team put the wounded American pilots in their homes for first-aid treatment, and then sent them back to the American airbase by using their horses and self-made stretchers. And friendship and love grew along with each of the rescue actions.

在驼峰飞行的日子里，云南陆良人民组织了一支战地志愿救援队——农民救护队。由于农民救护队的及时帮助，许多受伤的飞行员得以生还。志愿救护队把受伤的美国飞行员安排在自己的家中精心照料，再用骡马和自制担架把他们护送回美军基地。真情和友谊伴随着每一次的救护行动。

In a series of paintings, an unknown Hump pilot illustrated the rescue actions, and expressed his heartfelt gratitude to the Chinese people. This painting shows how the Chinese Yi minority people rescued him.

一位不知名的驼峰飞行员形象地用一组图画描绘了救护过程，表达他对中国百姓的感激之情。这组图画表现了中国彝族民众救护他的情景。

Air Dropped Propaganda leaflets

During those years in Kunming, posters such as this one were seen everywhere in the city and its rural areas.
在昆明的那些岁月里，这样的海报在城市和乡村中随处可见。

Lest We Forget
驼峰情

In the two small towns, Xiangyun and North Kansas, respectively in China and the United States, a monument has been erected for the same person. The hero's name was not only engraved in the two monuments, but also in the hearts of the peoples of the two towns.

在中国和美国的两座小城——祥云和北堪萨斯,都为同一个人建立了纪念标。两座纪念标永恒纪念的人都铭刻在两城人民的心中……

Xiangyun is in west Yunnan, China.
这个叫作祥云的小县城,位于中国云南省西部。

87

The Hump Route

At the traditional Chinese Qingming Festival that is celebrated each year on the 5th day of the 4th lunar month to cherish the ancestors and heroes, the peace-loving Xiangyun folks would mournfully stand first before a monument to pay tribute to an American martyr who is the hero in their hearts.

每年的 4 月 5 日是"清明节"，这是中国人祭奠祖先和英雄的日子。这一天，祥云人民总要先到这座纪念标前，缅怀他们心目中的一位美国英雄……

88

He was captain Robert H. Mooney.
他就是美军飞行员罗伯特·H·莫尼中尉。

Captain Mooney volunteered to come to Kunming, Yunnan, at a critical moment during the WWII. Stationed at Yunnanyi airport, Captain Mooney piloted a fighter plane to protect the airport and convoy the air freighters.

On December 26, 1942, the Japanese Army sent swarms of bombers to launch a sudden attack on Yunnanyi. Captain Mooney and his comrades took the lead in the counterattack, and smashed his P-40 into the enemy planes. It was indeed a bitter fight, and the gunfire burnt the sky over Xiangyun where Yunnanyi was located.

After shooting down an enemy plane, Captain Mooney saw an enemy plane ferociously heading straight for him. Fearlessly, Captain Mooney darted at the enemy plane head-on, crashed its left wing, and sent it tumbling to the ground.

Unfortunately, Captain Mooney's plane was engulfed in flames, and swirled toward Xiangyun Town. At the critical moment, CaptainMooney's only thought was to divert his plane from the town so as to avoid the catastrophic disaster that would not only kill Xiangyun people, but also ruin Yunnanyi airport. For the safety of Xiangyun Town that was right beneath him, Captain Mooney did not bale out right away. Instead, he courageously piloted his burning plane and managed to bring it away from the town.

Because of the fatal delay, Captain Mooney lost the necessary altitude for baling out. After he jumped out of his plane, the parachute failed to completely open. He hurtled to the ground, and the gale blew him off course by hundreds of meters. Seriously wounded,Captain Mooney might die at any moment. All the Xiangyun folks had seen that breathtakingly bitter air battle. As the fighter plane exploded on a hill behind the town, all the townspeople dashed out to rescue Captain Mooney.

莫尼中尉在第二次世界大战的危机关头，自愿来到云南昆明。他是一名战斗机驾驶员，驻守在"驼峰航线"重镇——祥云小镇旁的云南驿机场，担负着保卫机场和为运输机护航的军事任务。

1942 年 12 月 26 日，日军部署大批轰炸机突然袭击云南驿机场，莫尼中尉和他的战友率先驾驶 P-40 战斗机，冲入日军机群。空战异常惨烈，战火映红了祥云的上空。

莫尼中尉顽强击落了一架敌机后，另一架敌机向莫尼中尉迎面冲来。莫尼中尉奋不顾身，撞向敌机，敌机左机翼被撞断坠毁。

莫尼中尉战机不幸起火，急速地向祥云县城坠去。在生死存亡关头，他想到如果飞机坠落在祥云城中，将会造成毁灭性的灾难，而且会殃及云南驿机场。为了不使飞机坠入祥云县城，莫尼中尉没有及时跳伞，顽强地控制着飞机，飞离祥云城。

这时，莫尼中尉失去了跳伞的必要高度，跳机之后，降落伞没有完全打开。莫尼中尉重重地摔在田野上，被刮着的大风拖出了几百米远，伤势严重，生命垂危。祥云城的民众目睹了这一惊心动魄的场面，当战机在小城后山爆炸的时候，全城民众纷纷急速出城抢救。

When the dying Captain was rushed to the operating table, Dong Jiyuan, a well-known Yunnan doctor, did his best and used all the best medicine he had on him, but failed to save him. Captain Mooney died on the night of the same day. The entire Xiangyun Town mourned the American hero…

当莫尼中尉血肉模糊地被送到手术台的时候，云南名医董济元倾其所有，用上全部珍存最好的进口药品，抢救莫尼中尉。终因伤势过重，莫尼中尉当晚牺牲在祥云。祥云城举城悲痛……

To show their eternal gratitude and respect for Captain Mooney's heroic deeds, the Xiangyun people voluntarily donated money to build a monument for him. Five months later, the "Monument of Robert H. Mooney, Captain of the American Air Force" was completed. The 14th Air Force and Xiangyun people jointly held a solemn ceremony to unveil the monument.

小城民众为了表达永恒的怀念之情和纪念莫尼中尉拯救祥云的壮举，自发地捐款捐物，决定为莫尼中尉建一座纪念标。5 个月后，"美国空军莫尼中尉殉职纪念标"建成，美国第 14 航空队官兵和祥云城的民众，共同举行了大规模落成典礼。

50 years later, Captain Mooney's sister Ena L. Davis came to Xiangyun to see the old people who witnessed the historic episode, and their offspring.

50年后，莫尼中尉的妹妹埃娜·L·戴维斯来到了祥云，看望见证了这段历史的老人们及他们的后代。

Having stayed for a while with the local people, Ena was deeply touched and chose two passages from a hymn of Rudyard Kipling, the Ballad of East and West, to Xiangyun folks:

埃娜·L·戴维斯与祥云人民共同生活一段时间后，她感慨万分，从诗人吉卜琳的一首赞美诗中节选了两段，赠与祥云人民。

Oh East is East, and West is West, and never
The twain shall meet,
Till Earth and Sky stand presently at God's
Great Judgement Seat;
But there is neither East nor West, Border,
Nor Breed, nor Birth,
When two strong men stand face to face, tho'
They come from the end of the earth!

The tumult and the shouting dies —
The captains and the kings depart —
Still stands thine ancient sacrifice,
A humble and contrite heart,
Lord God of Hosts, be with us yet,
Lest we forget!

哦！东方在东方，西方在西方，
两方不相遇，直至天和地，
站在上帝的面前，接受最后的洗礼。
可是，哪里还有东方、西方，甚至国界、种族，
两个强健的民族自地球的这方和那方，
走到一起，面对着面！

喧嚣和欢乐都已平息，
国王和首领也已逝去，
只有您的勇士啊，依然屹立，
以一颗平凡宁静的心。
全能的主啊！求您与我们共存，
为的是我们永不磨灭的记忆……
东方不再是东方，西方不再是西方！

Returning to the Hump
回访驼峰

In May 1991, the Chinese and American peoples laid down the foundation for the Hump Flight Memorial in Kunming, Yunnan.
1991 年 5 月，中美两国在云南昆明共同为建造"驼峰飞行纪念碑"奠基。

On May 28, 1995, a plane with veteran US Hump pilots landed at the Wujiaba Airport in Kunming.
1995 年 5 月 28 日，美国驼峰老飞行员乘坐的飞机降落在昆明巫家坝机场。

In 1995, the 50th anniversary of the victory of the Anti-Japanese War, a World War II Hump Flight Commemoration Ceremony was held in front of the Hump Flight Memorial in Kunming.

1995 年是抗日战争胜利 50 周年,中美"二战驼峰飞行纪念仪式"在昆明的"驼峰飞行纪念碑"前举行。

The veteran hump pilots, both Chinese and American, paid their respects to the Memorial to commemorate the soldiers who offered their lives for world peace. They recalled the history that the peoples of the two countries made together and cherished the friendship that has lasted until today.

中美驼峰老飞行员在"驼峰飞行纪念碑"前致敬并敬献花圈，缅怀为世界和平而献出生命的驼峰勇士，回顾中美人民共同走过的历史和延续至今的友谊。

On March 31, 2002, White Stevens, a veteran pilot of the American 14th Air Force and his comrades re-visited the Hump. They took a special tour to Kunming, and went to the Monument of the Hump Flights to pay respect to all the people who had contributed to the "Hump Flights".

2002 年 3 月 31 日，美国老飞行员怀特·史蒂文斯一行重返驼峰，专程来到中国云南昆明的"驼峰飞行纪念碑"前，向所有为"驼峰飞行"做出过贡献的人们致敬。

The Hump Flight Memorial is a monument to the mutual trust and sincere cooperation between China and the United States in pursuit of common interests. It is also a monument of peace and friendship between the two peoples.

"驼峰飞行纪念碑"是中美两国为了共同的利益、相互信赖、真诚合作的丰碑，是中美两国人民热爱和平、发展友谊的丰碑！

Col. C.L.

陈纳德和美国志愿航空队

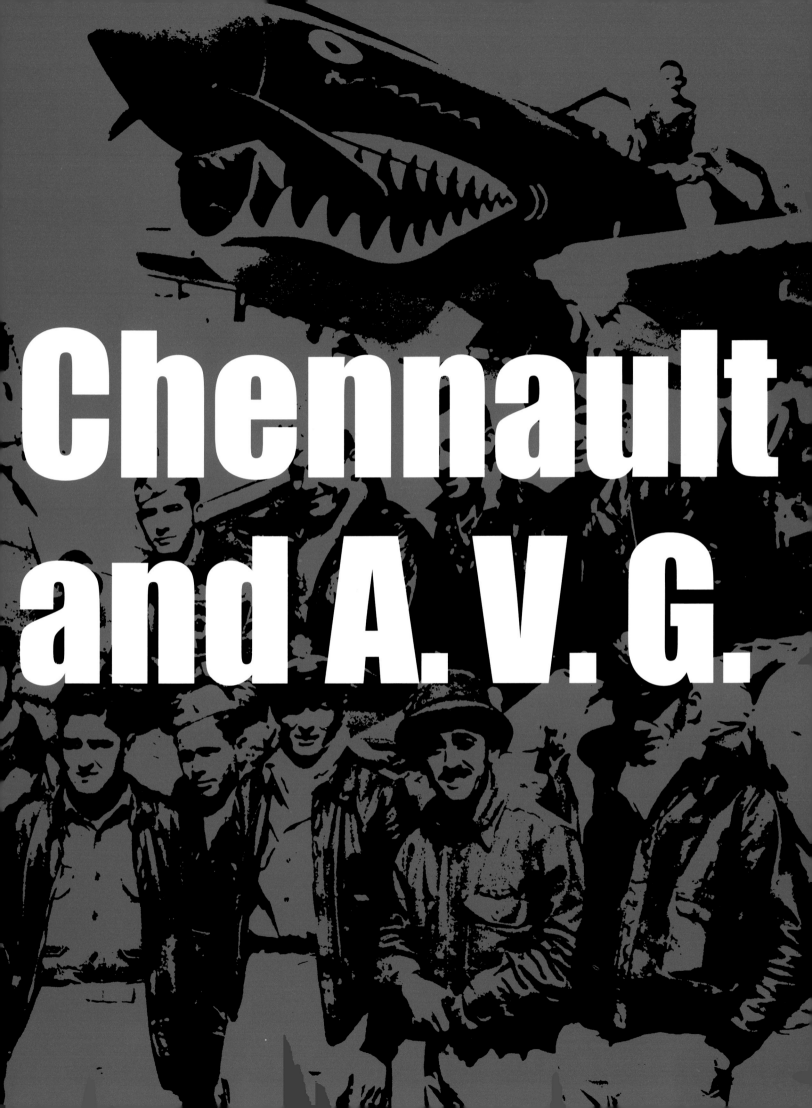

Chennault and A. V. G.

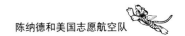

There was an air corps composed of volunteers who came from the other side of the ocean to the China, Burma and India War Theatr to support the Anti-Japanese War. This corps accomplished their mission successfully in the fight against the Japanese air force and of protecting the Burma Road.

有一支志愿航空部队为支援抗日战争，从遥远的大洋彼岸投入到中缅印战区，在对日军航空兵作战和保卫滇缅公路的战斗中屡建奇功。

This army, which was the American Volunteer Group (A.V.G.), was called the " Flying Tigers" by the Chinese people.
这支部队就是被中国百姓誉为"飞虎队"的美国志愿航空队。

On July 10, 1941, the first batch of A.V.G., more than 200 people came to China from San Francisco. On August 1, the A.V.G. of the Chinese Air Force was founded and set up base in Kunming of Yunnan Province.　The commander was Colonel Claire L. Chennault.

1941 年 7 月 10 日，"美国志愿航空队"的首批人员 200 多人从美国旧金山前往中国。8 月 1 日，"中国空军美国志愿航空队"正式成立，司令部设在昆明，司令陈纳德。

The original "Flying Tigers" patch of the AVG was designed in early 1942 by Walt Disney Studios. A Bengal tiger with wings is shown soaring out of a V for Victory.

"飞虎队"的标志原型由美国迪斯尼公司在 1942 年设计。一只展翼的孟加拉虎从代表着胜利的"V"字中飞扑而出。

The "Flying Tigers" underwent changes as it developed. First, it was on active service on July 4, 1942 and became the 10th Air Force China Air Task Force; then in March 1943, it became the 14th Air Force.

"飞虎队"进行过两次改编。1942 年 7 月 4 日纳入现役,改称"美国陆军第 10 航空队驻华空军特遣队";1943 年 3 月,又改编为"美国陆军第 14 航空队"。

At this time of war, there was a sort of deep love between the Flying Tigers and the local people of Yunnan. So, they got along with each other very well.

在那战争的岁月里，"飞虎队"队员与云南百姓和睦相处，情深义重。

Also, they enjoyed themselves between battles.
在战斗的间隙里,"飞虎队"队员们自娱自乐。

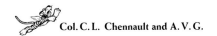

In order to fight against the Japanese air force more effectively, the "Flying Tigers" set up Wujiaba airport in Kunming, and Luliang airport to the east, Yanggai airport and Chengkung airport to the south, Baoshan airport and Yunnanyi airport to the west of Kunming.

为了更有效地对日作战，"飞虎队"在中国云南昆明设有巫家坝机场，在昆明东部设有陆良机场，在昆明南部设有羊街机场、呈贡机场，在昆明西部设有保山机场、云南驿机场等。

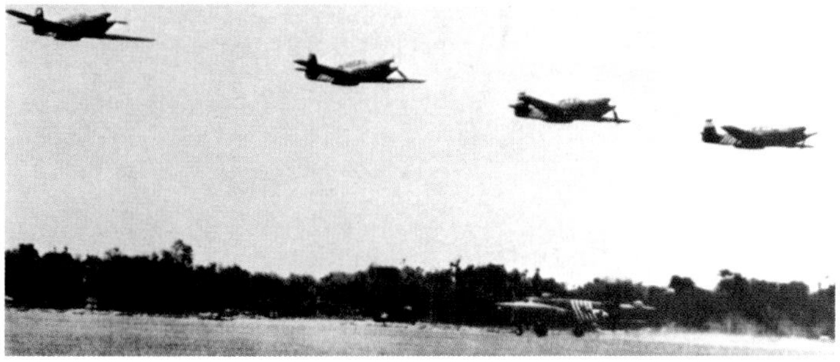

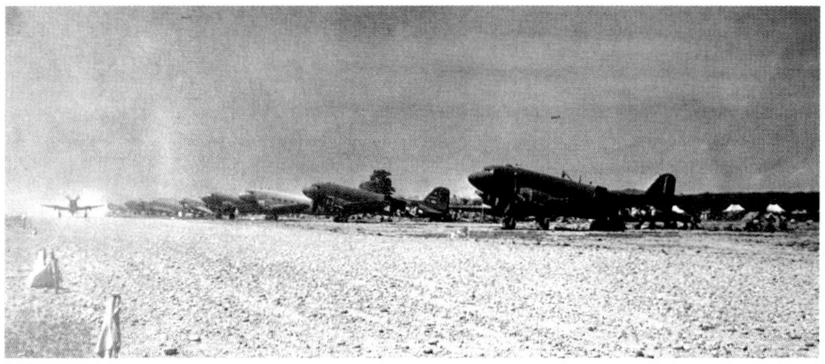

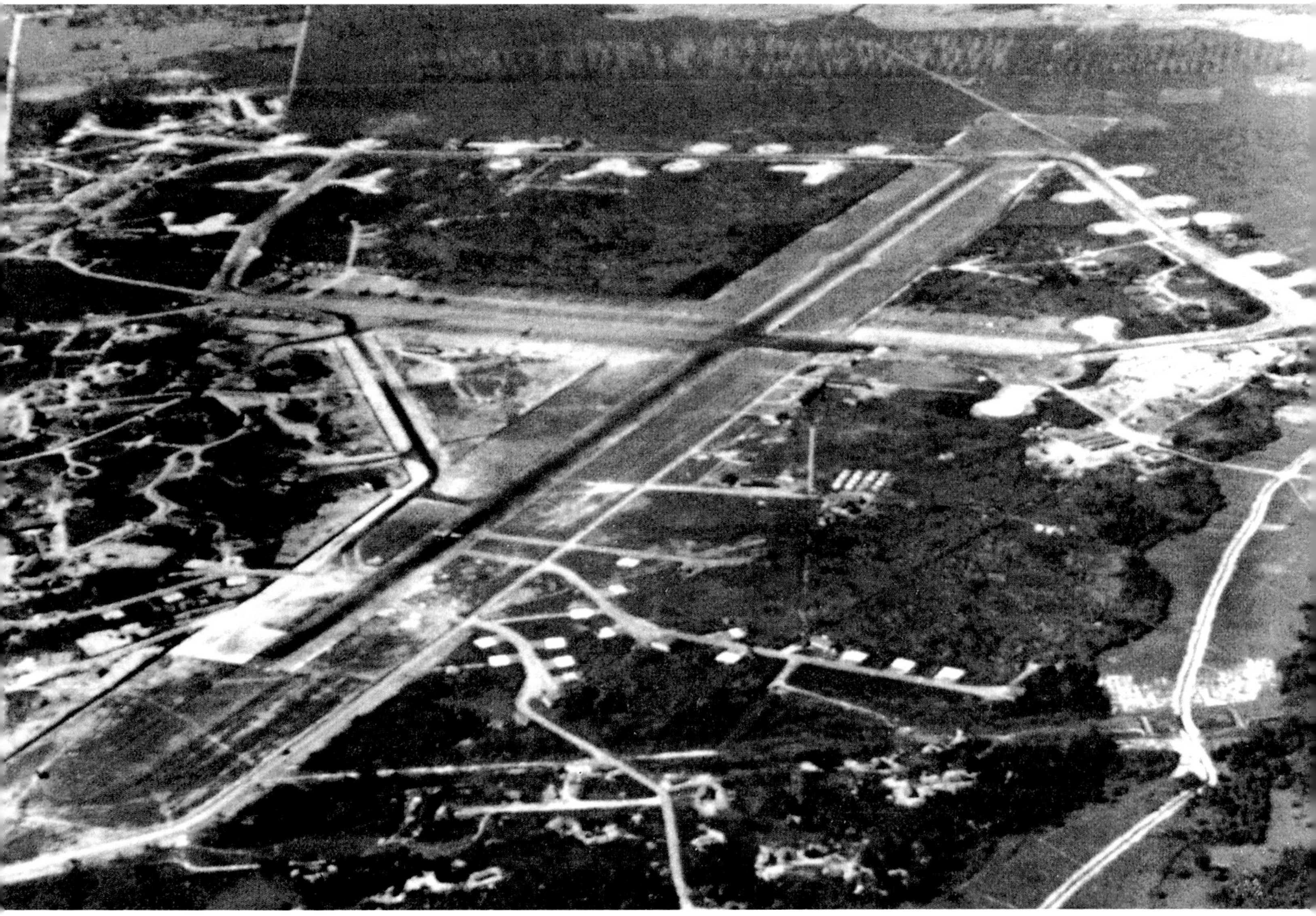

The more airports were still under construction.
更多的机场还在修建中。

114

On December 20, 1941, 24 P-40 fighter planes took off from Wujiaba airport in Kunming to fight against 10 enemy planes. It turned out that nine of the enemy planes were shot down and the other one was damaged with no loss to the Flying Tigers.

1941 年 12 月 20 日,"飞虎队" 24 架 P-40 型战斗机从昆明巫家坝机场凌空而起,狙击 10 架来犯日机,取得了击落敌机 9 架、击伤 1 架,而自身无一损失的战绩。

On April 28, 1942, this air corps made another brilliant achievement in an air battle over Lashio in Burma, when 22 enemy planes were shot down, but the "Flying Tigers" suffered no losses.

1942 年 4 月 28 日，"飞虎队"在缅甸腊戌再次创下了击落日军飞机 22 架，自身无一损失的辉煌战绩……

The 14th Air Force had shot down 2,600 Japanese planes, destroyed or damaged 2,230,000t enemy merchant ships, 44 warships and more than 13,000 inland river ships with a weight below 100t each, with the loss of 500 planes of their own. They also shot 66,700 Japanese soldiers.

第 14 航空队战果辉煌，以损失 500 架飞机的代价，共击落日军飞机 2600 架，击沉或重创 223 万吨敌商船，44 艘军舰，13000 艘 100 吨以下的内河船只，击毙日军官兵 66700 名。

Authorized by William Pawley in 1945, Raymond Neilson painted portraits of combat heroes of the Flying Tigers, whose heroic deeds embodied those of all the Flying Tigers' airmen.

1945年威廉·保利授权雷蒙德·尼尔逊创作"飞虎队"战斗英雄的油画，他们的英雄故事是"飞虎英雄"的缩影。

Marion Baugh died in line of duty near Kunming, January 4, 1942. In a letter to the Chinese, Marion's mother wrote, "I gave to China a young man who knew no fear. Nor did he fail to heed the call of duty.These principles and ideals were handed down to him from generations…"

莫里森·鲍，1942年1月4日执行任务时在昆明牺牲。莫里森的母亲在给中方的一封信中写道："我献给中国的是一个英勇无畏的儿子，他从未辜负自己的职责。他继承发扬了我们家族世代相传的精神和理想……"

Allen Christman, a flight leader, had his plane damaged in a fight with the enemy aircraft, and bailed out. He was killed by three 1-97 Nakajimas strafing him over the rice paddies south of Rangoon, January 23, 1942. Christman was a cartoonist-assistant to Milton Caniff before he joined the A.V.G.

艾兰·克里斯特曼，飞行中队长。在1942年1月23日的空战中，战机被敌击伤，跳伞后在仰光南部的稻田中被3架日机射杀。参加美国志愿航空队前，他曾任漫画家米尔顿·凯尼夫的助手。

Thomas Cole Jr., a Golden Gloves champion from Pensacola, Florida, was killed on a reconnaissance mission over Moulmein, Burma, January 30, 1942.

托马斯·科尔，曾是佛罗里达州蓬萨克拉的高尔夫球冠军。1942 年 1 月 30 日在缅甸毛淡棉上空执行侦察飞行任务时牺牲。

John Donovan, lacking one "victory" of becoming an ace, was shot down by flak in a raid over Hanoi, May 12, 1942.

约翰·多诺万，仅差一次胜利记录就可成为空战英雄。1942 年 5 月 12 日，其战机在空袭河内时被敌炮火击落。

Max Hammer, had studied aeronautical engineering at Louisiana State University. He lost control of his airplane in a monsoon over Burma on September 22, 1941, and crashed, the first casualty of the A.V.G.

麦克斯·海莫尔，曾在路易斯安那州学过航空工程学。1941 年 9 月 22 日，在缅甸的一次季风中飞机失控坠毁。这是美国志愿航空队首次人员伤亡。

Louis Hoffman, a flight leader, engaged five enemy planes before he was shot down over Rangoon on January 26, 1942. He was 44 years old, the oldest pilot flying with the A.V.G. and one of the best.

路易斯·霍夫曼，飞行中队长。1942 年 1 月 26 日，在仰光空战中与 5 架敌机拼杀，后被击落牺牲，时年 44 岁。他是美国志愿航空队年龄最大、也是最优秀的飞行员之一。

Thomas Jones left his 20-year-old bride, an expectant mother, to join the A.V.G. He was killed in a fight over Kunming on May 16, 1942.

托马斯·琼斯，离别 20 岁、身怀六甲的爱妻参加了美国志愿航空队。1942 年 5 月 16 日，在昆明上空的一次战斗中牺牲。

Robert Litte shot down 10 enemy fighters and bombers before he was shot down over the Salween River.

罗伯特·里特，1942 年 5 月 22 日在萨尔温江上空被击落而牺牲，此前他共击落了 10 架敌机。

Neil Martin engaged the enemy over Rangoon on December 23, 1941. The fire from several enemy bombers converged on him, and he was shot down and killed, the first American Volunteer to die in combat over Burma.

尼尔·马丁，1941 年 12 月 23 日在仰光上空与敌机交战时，遭数架敌机围攻，被击落而牺牲。他是在缅甸空域牺牲的第一位美国志愿航空队飞行员。

Robert Sandell, who shot down 5 enemy planes in two days, was killed on February 7, 1942.

罗伯特·桑德尔，创下了两天击落 5 架敌机的纪录，1942 年 2 月 7 日牺牲。

Frank Schiel Jr. destroyed seven enemy planes before being shot down in China, December 22, 1943.

弗兰克·席尔，1943 年 12 月 22 日在中国被击落，牺牲前共击落敌机 7 架。

Frank Swartz died in a British hospital "under the combat skies of Poona".

弗兰克·史华兹，在印度浦那的空战中受伤，后在一家英国医院中身亡。

John Newkrik had 12 confirmed victories. He was killed on March 24, 1942.

约翰·纽克里克，有 12 次空战胜利纪录，1942 年 3 月 24 日牺牲。

John Petach Jr. married Emma Foster, an army nurse attached to the A.V.G. He was killed on July 10, 1942. A daughter was born to Mrs. Petach on February 17, 1943.

约翰·彼泰克，与美国志愿航空队女护士爱玛·福斯特结婚，1942 年 7 月 10 日牺牲。1943 年 2 月 17 日，女儿出生。

Ben Foshee，a wing man， died on May 4， 1942 of wounds received during an enemy bombing raid near Baoshan in western Yunnan Province.

本·福什，僚机飞行员。1942 年 5 月 4 日敌机轰炸滇西保山时受伤，后不治身亡。

Henry Gilbert，a former Navy dive-bomber and patrol pilot, was shot down in aerial combat over Rangoon, December 23, 1941.

亨利·吉尔伯特，曾为海军轰炸巡航机飞行员。1941 年 12 月 23 日，在仰光上空的空战中被击落而牺牲。

Lacy Mangleburg, a Georgian, was killed on December 23, 1941 in a training flight.

莱西·蒙格尔伯格，乔治亚州人，1941 年 12 月 23 日在一次飞行训练中遇难。

Rescuing

营救杜利特尔轰炸机队

the Doolittle's Bombers

Lieutenant Colonel James Harold Doolittle.
杜利特尔中校

After the Pacific War launched, under orders, Lt. Col. James Harold Doolittle led 16 B-25 bombers from the aircraft carrier *USS Hornet* to bomb Tokyo and other Japanese cities on April 18, 1942.
太平洋战争爆发后，1942 年 4 月 18 日，杜利特尔中校奉命率领 16 架 B-25 型轰炸机从"大黄蜂"号航空母舰上起飞，对日本东京等城市进行轰炸。

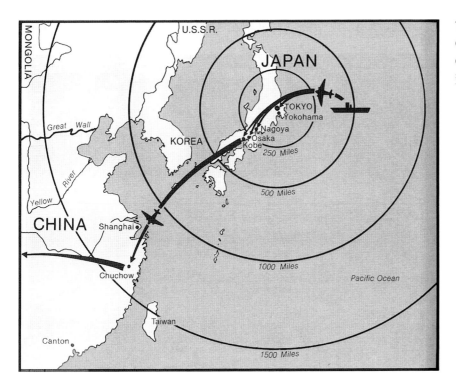

US bombers were scheduled to land at the Quzhou(Chuchow) Airport in Zhejiang Province, China.

轰炸机队计划降落在中国浙江的衢州机场

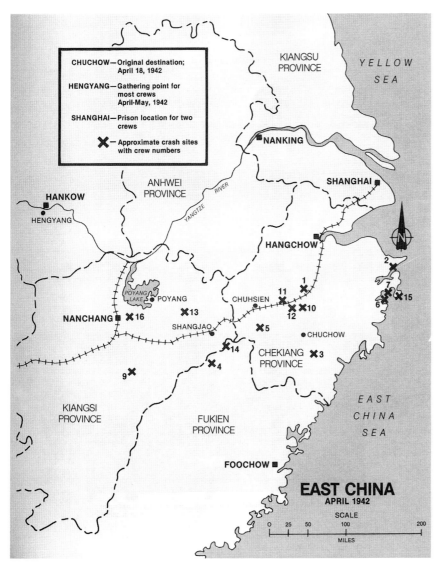

CHUCHOW—Original destination; April 18, 1942

HENGYANG—Gathering point for most crews April-May, 1942

SHANGHAI—Prison location for two crews

✘ — Approximate crash sites with crew numbers

EAST CHINA
APRIL 1942

SCALE
0   25   50   100   200
MILES

After the mission, however, they lost contact with the ground command station, and were unable to return to where they should land. Fifteen of the bombers crashed in China's Anhui and Zhejiang provinces. Five of the 75 US crewmen died, eight others were captured by the Japanese, and the remaining 62 were rescued by the Chinese civilians.

机队完成任务后,因与地面失去联络,其中15架飞机在中国浙江、安徽等省坠毁。75名飞行员中,除5人丧生和8人被日军捕俘外,其余62人被中国百姓救助,安全脱险。

A duplicate copy of the map of East China in 1942 as supplied by US pilots in 1989. Where the 15 US bombers landed or crashed are marked accurately. (Note: HENGYANG's location is wrongly marked.)

美国飞行员1989年提供的一份1942年华东地图复制品,上面标示了美军15架飞机的坠落地点。(注:此图中"衡阳"位置疑误)

129

No. 1 Bomber

1号机

杜利特尔所在的 1 号机坠落在中国浙江省和安徽省交界处的昊天关。5 名飞行员弃机跳伞后,降落在浙江省临安县境内的天目山一带。第二天,几位青年学员发现了在稻田水碓里露宿了一夜的杜利特尔,并将他护送到浙西行署。其他飞行员在粗通英文的小学教员朱学三以及村民张根荣等人护送下和杜利特尔会合。

Lt. Col. Doolittle's No. 1 bomber crashed in Haotianguan, where Zhejiang Province meets Anhui Province. Five pilots parachuted and landed in the Tianmushan area in Lin'an County, Zhejiang Province. Lt. Col. Doolittle stayed overnight in a water-powered trip-hammer in a paddy field until he was found by several young students the next day, and escorted to the Western Zhejiang Administration. There, he was joined by his fellow crewmen who were escorted here by Zhu Xuesan, a primary school teacher who could speak some English, and certain villagers including Zhang Gengrong.

Wreckage of the No.1 US bomber.
1 号机残骸

Lt. Col. Doolittle posing in front of the
wreckage of his bomber.
杜利特尔在飞机残骸前

Lt. Col. Doolittle and his crewmen having a picture taken with the Chinese friends who helped them in Lin'an.
杜利特尔及机组人员与帮助他们的中国朋友在临安的合影

Zhang Gengrong(the middle), now an old man, recalled how Lt. Richard E. Cole was rescued.

张根荣老人(中)回忆当年救助飞行员科尔的情景

No. 7 Bomber

7号机

7号机坠落在中国浙江省三门县海域。当地百姓把 5 名受伤的飞行员送至附近海游镇做简单包扎，然后用轿子将伤势较重的 4 名飞行员火速抬往当时医疗条件最好的临海恩泽医局救治。医生陈慎言和闻讯赶来的美国军医怀特为伤员劳逊成功实施了截肢手术。为照顾他们的生活，还请来两名英国修女当翻译，做西餐给他们吃。陈慎言医师护送 4 名受伤飞行员到广西桂林。

No. 7 bomber fell into the sea under the jurisdiction of Sanmen County, Zhejiang Province. Local villagers took the five US crew to Haiyou Town to have their wounds simply dressed. Four of the five, who were seriously wounded, were rushed in sedan chairs to the Linhai Enze Medical Bureau, where better medical facilities were available. Chen Shenyan, a medical doctor, and US military medical doctor Lt. Thomas R. White, who rushed there when told the news, succeeded in performing a limb amputation on Ted W. Lawson. Two British nuns were invited to be his interpreters and cook Western food for him. Dr. Chen Shenyan then escorted the four other US wounded crewmen to Guilin in Guangxi.

Portrait of Chen Shenyan.
陈慎言像

Portrait of Ted W. Lawson.
劳逊像

Old site of the Enze Medical Bureau.
恩泽医局旧址

No. 11 Bomber

11号机

11 号机在中国浙江和安徽两省交界处的山区坠毁。当地百姓将 5 名飞行员送往安徽省歙县。在那里，当翻译曾健培问他们有什么需要时，飞行员波尔茨说需要一瓶啤酒。在当时，啤酒是非常稀罕的东西。让波尔茨倍感意外的是，曾健培居然为他搞来了一瓶"上海"牌啤酒。在回忆中，波尔茨将这瓶啤酒称为"一生中喝到的最可口的啤酒".

No.11 bomber crashed in a mountainous area on the border of Zhejiang and Anhui provinces.Five US crew were escorted to Shexian County in Anhui Province.When Zeng Jianpei,an interpreter, asked them about their needs, S/Sgt. William L. Birch said he wanted a bottle of beer. Beer was rarely found then. To his surprise, however, Zeng found him a Shanghai brand bottle of beer.Recalling this segment of history, S/Sgt. Birch later said that bottle of beer was "the tastiest beer I have ever tasted in my life."

Zeng Jianpei and Wei Hanmin who involved in rescuing the American pilots(50 years ago and 50 years after).
参与救助美国飞行员的曾健培和魏汉民 50 年前、后的合影

At the ceremony held in 1992 in the United States to mark the 50th anniversary of the Doolittle Raid, Lt. Frank A. Kappeler, a crew member of No.11 bomber, presented Zeng Jianpei with 50 bottles of beer.
1992 年，在杜利特尔轰炸行动 50 周年纪念活动上，11 号机组的飞行员开普勒推出 50 瓶啤酒回赠曾健培。

No. 15 Bomber

15号机

15 号机坠落在中国浙江象山南田大沙洋面,5 名机组人员在当地渔民的帮助下,安全通过日军封锁线。

No. 15 bomber crashed into the Dasha Sea, Nantian, Xiangshan, Zhejiang Province. With the help of local fishermen, the five crewmen safely sneaked through the Japanese blockade.

American pilots having a picture taken with their Chinese friends.
美军飞行员与中国朋友在告别集会上的合影

No. 3 Bomber

3号机

3号机坠落在中国浙江遂昌县境内，4名飞行员被当地百姓营救。遂昌农民刘芳桥边扶边背，从早上6点一直到晚上7点，走了30多里山路，把飞行员查尔斯·欧祖克送到安全地带。飞行员雷兰德·法克特在坠落时丧生。当地百姓按中国人的习俗，夜里在山上守尸，以防尸体被野兽吃掉，后用上好棺木入殓，运至衢州机场。

No. 3 bomber fell in Suichang County, Zhejiang Province. Four US crewmen were found and rescued by local people. Liu Fangqiao, a peasant, managed to carry Lt. Charles J. Ozuk Jr. to a safe place, and the trip, extending some 15 km through the mountains, lasted from six in the morning until seven in the evening. Cpl. Leland D. Faktor, another crewman, died in the crash. Local people stood vigil over the body overnight in accordance with Chinese tradition and also to prevent it from being eaten by wild animals. The body was then placed in a coffin for shipment to Quzhou Airport.

Segments of crashed US bomber No.3.
3 号机残片

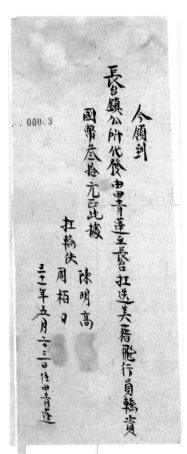

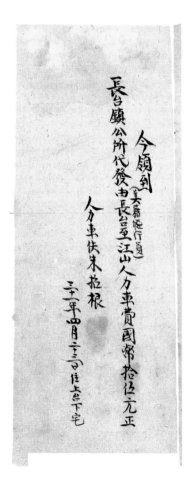

Receipts showing fees paid for carrying the American pilots in sedan chairs or rickshaws.
护送美国飞行员的轿资、人力车费收条

141

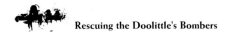
No. 2 Bomber

2号机

Crewmen of No.2 US bomber with Tung-Sheng Liu (third right), a Chinese man involved in the rescue work.

2 号机组飞行员与中国营救人员刘同声（右三）等合影

The rescued US crew.

被救飞行员合影

C 25758

营救杜利特尔轰炸机队

The Chinese used sedan chairs to carry
wounded American crewmen.
中国人用轿子护送受伤的飞行员

SOS letters written by US pilot.
美国飞行员手书的求救书信

143

Cost

代价

1942 年 5 月 15 日至 8 月中旬，为摧毁浙赣两省中国空军机场，日军集中 9 个师以上的兵力，发动大规模的浙赣战役。1942 年 5 月 15 日，日军对杜利特尔轰炸机队主要降落地点发动大规模进攻，并使用了细菌武器。

为救助美国飞行员，中国百姓遭受日军的残酷迫害，付出了血的代价。飞虎将军陈纳德回忆录中详细记载了日军的残暴行径："在这次为时三个月的战役中，日军把战争的矛头直指中国东部的中心地带，在两百平方英里的范围内，实行'三光'政策，犁毁机场，并把所有协助杜利特尔轰炸机队的嫌疑人统统杀掉。美国飞机经过的村庄的全村村民，不分老小，全被杀光，房屋全被烧掉……二十五万中国士兵和平民，死于这场三个月的战役中。中国人为杜利特尔的轰炸付出了惨重代价，但他们并不抱怨。在后来的战斗岁月里，他们也从未停止过对那些降落在日本占领区的美国飞行员进行帮助。"

From May 15 to mid-August of 1942, the Japanese troops composed of nine divisions launched a large-scale sweep against airports in Zhejiang and Anhui provinces. On May 15, 1942, the Japanese troops attacked the area where Lt. Col. Doolittle's bombers fell, and even resorted to use of bacterial weapons.

For their help to the downed American bomber crews, the Chinese suffered cruel suppression by the Japanese invaders and paid with their blood. *Way of A Fighter* written by Flying Tigers General Claire Chennault recorded in detail the atrocities of the Japanese troops: "During the three-month battle, the Japanese troops directed the spearhead of war at the central part of eastern China. In an area measuring 200 square miles, they followed the three-all policy, razing the airport and killing all suspected to have helped Lt. Col. Doolittle and his men. All the villagers, old and young, in the area where the US bombers crashed, were slaughtered and their houses burnt down.... Some 250,000 Chinese soldiers and civilians died in the three-month battle. The Chinese paid heavily for the American bombing raid, but they had no complaints and they never ceased to aid and support American pilots who were forced to land in Japanese controlled areas."

Japanese troops entering Quzhou City.
日军部队进入衢州城

Name list of Yiwu residents killed by the Japanese in bacteria campaign.
义乌市侵华日军细菌战受害者名单

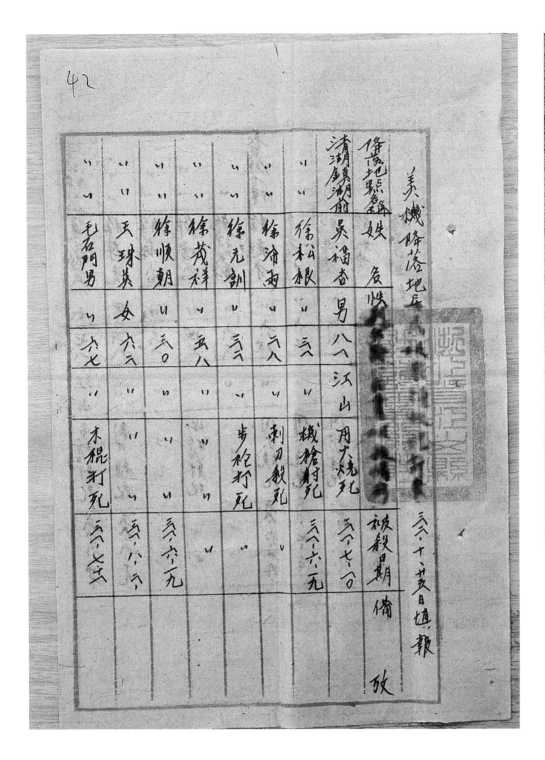
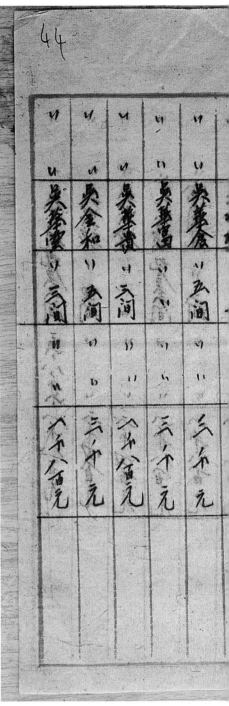

Tables showing the losses incurred by Changtai Town and Qinghu Town of Zhejiang Province (where some of the US bombers crashed) by the Japanese invaders: 27 people killed, and 400,000 Chinese yuan worth of housing burnt down.

美国飞行员降落地浙江省江山县长台镇和清湖镇居民被日军残杀暨房屋财产损失表，计被杀害者 27 人，房屋被焚毁等财产损失 40 万元。

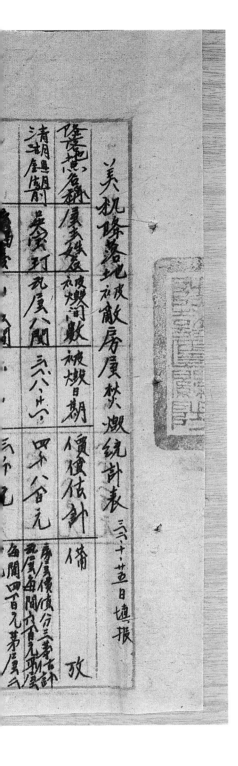

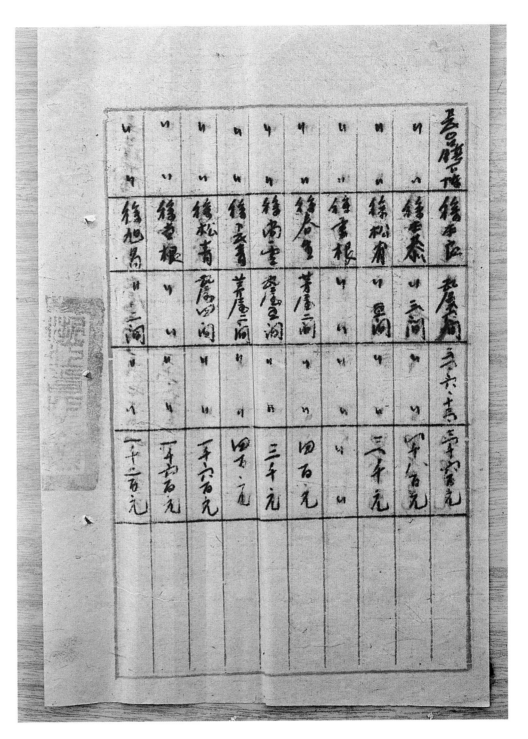

In September 1990, Bryan Moon, a friend of Lt. Col. Doolittle's, who was the former vice-president of US Northwest Airlines, organized a group of five to visit those people in Zhejiang and Anhui Provinces involved in rescuing the American pilots.

On March 13, 1992, five Chinese senior citizens—Chen Shenyan, Zhu Xuesan, Zeng Jianpei, Zhao Xiaobao and Liu Fangqiao—attended the ceremony in the United States to mark the 50th anniversary of the Doolittle Raid. They went in response to the invitation of the Doolittle Bombers Association. During their 10-day visit, the five showed up at several large-scale public activities and received warm hospitality from the Americans. US President George Bush sent them a letter of greeting, and US Defense Secretary Dick Cheney met them in his office. The American mass media covered the visit in detail.

At a ceremony to mark the 50th anniversary of the Doolittle Raid, US President George Bush spoke highly of this segment of history: "On this special occasion, we also salute those good people in China who, following the raid and without regard for their own well-being, provided shelter and protection for wounded Americans. Thanks to such humanitarian efforts, these Raiders were able to find their way back to safety. Although half a century has passed since their gold strike in the name of freedom, the Doolittle Raiders continue to inspire respect and awe among the American peopoe .We will never forget their extraordinary contribution — nor that of their Chinese rescuers — to the worthy cause of liberty and justice."

In 1994, Moon once again organized a search for wreckage of the crashed US bombers in the coastal area in Zhejiang, and was the searchers reunited with those involved in the rescuing mission, including Zhu Xuesan, Chen Shenyan, Zhao Xiaobao and Wang Xiaofu.

1990 年 9 月，杜利特尔的朋友、原美国西北航空公司副总裁穆恩组织一支 5 人考察团来到中国浙江、安徽等地寻访当年参加营救美国飞行员的中国老人。

1992 年 3 月 13 日，5 位中国老人陈慎言、朱学三、曾健培、赵小宝、刘芳桥应杜利特尔轰炸机队协会的邀请，赴美参加"杜利特尔行动" 50 周年纪念活动。在访问美国的 10 多天时间里，5 位老人出席了多次大型见面活动，受到美国人民的种种礼遇和热情款待；美国总统乔治·布什致信问候，国防部长切尼在办公室接见了他们；美国媒体进行了大量报道。

在"杜利特尔行动" 50 周年纪念活动上，美国总统乔治·布什对这段历史作出了高度评价："在突袭以后，那些善良的中国人不顾自己的安危，为我们的飞行员提供掩护并为他们疗伤。在这具有特殊意义的时刻，我们也向他们表示崇高的敬意，感谢他们作出的人道主义努力，是他们的帮助才使我们的飞行员们能够安全返回。杜利特尔行动虽然已经过去半个世纪了，但这些英雄们一直受到美国人民的敬仰和尊重。我们永远不会忘记他们所作出的伟大功勋，也永远不会忘记为自由和正义事业作出贡献的中国人。"

1994 年，穆恩再次组织人员来浙江沿海寻找当年坠落入海的飞机残骸，并与朱学三、陈慎言、赵小宝、王小富等当年参加救助的中国百姓重聚。

US inspection group posing for a picture in 1990 in front of the inn where Lt. Col Doolittle stayed.
1990 年，美国考察团在杜利特尔曾留宿的旅馆门前合影。

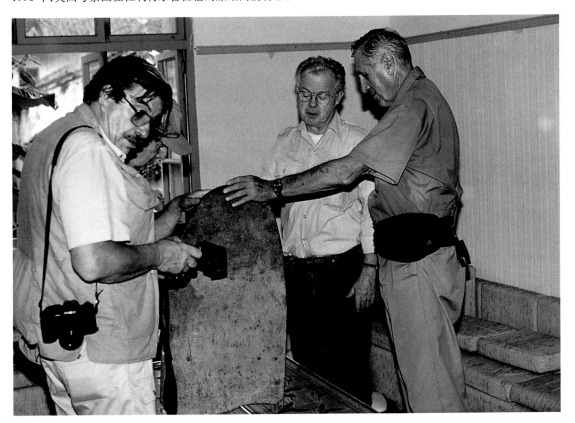

Handover of the wreckages of No.1 bomber.
移交 1 号机残骸

THE WHITE HOUSE

WASHINGTON

March 17, 1992

I am delighted to send warm greetings to my fellow
World War II veterans and to all those who are gathered
in Red Wing, Minnesota, to commemorate the 50th
Anniversary of the Doolittle Raiders' historic mission.
Special greetings to the survivors of that heroic
mission and to the Chinese citizens who protected our
downed air crews.

When then Lieutenant Colonel Doolittle and his squadron
of B-25 bombers accomplished their extraordinary feat
on April 18, 1942, they helped to lead the way for the
many victories that the United States and its allies
would later achieve in the Pacific Theatre. Colonel
Doolittle and his men showed that the United States and
its Allies could carry the battle to the enemy. The
success of the Raiders motivated and inspired our Armed
Forces for months, and even years, afterward.

On this special occasion, we also salute those good
people in China who, following the raid and without
regard for their own well-being, provided shelter and
protection for wounded Americans. Thanks to such
humanitarian efforts, these Raiders were able to find
their way back to safety.

Although half a century has passed since their bold
strike in the name of freedom, the Doolittle Raiders
continue to inspire respect and awe among the American
people. We will never forget their extraordinary
contribution -- nor that of their Chinese rescuers --
to the worthy cause of libery and justice.

Barbara joins me in sending best wishes for an
enjoyable reunion. God bless you.

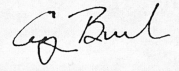

Letter from US President George Bush to the 50th anniversary of the 30 Seconds Over Tokyo Raid in 1992.
1992 年，美国总统乔治·布什致"东京上空 30 秒"行动 50 周年庆典活动贺信

Five Chinese senior citizens—Chen Shenyan (first row, third left), Zhao Xiaobao (fourth left), Zhu Xuesan (fifth left), Liu Fangqiao (sixth left) and Zeng Jianpei (seventh left)—having their picture taken with the US crewmen they rescued in front of the White House.
5 位老人陈慎言（前排左 3）、赵小宝（左 4）、朱学三（左 5）、刘芳桥（左 6）、曾健培（左 7）和曾被他们救助过的美国飞行员在白宫前合影

US Defense Secretary Dick Cheney meeting with the five Chinese in his office.
美国国防部长切尼在办公室接见 5 位老人

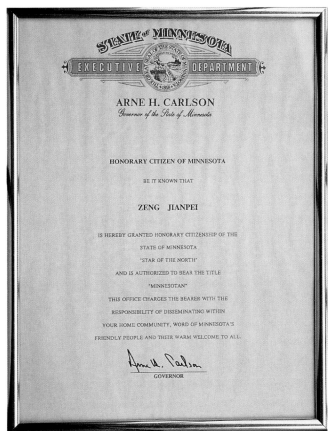

The Governor of Minnesota issuing certificates as honorary residents to the five Chinese.
美国明尼苏达州州长向 5 位中国老人颁发荣誉市民证书

Program Introduction

Retired Colonel "Hank" Potter, Navigator on "Jimmy" Doolittle's lead bomber for the 1942 first U.S. bombing raid on Japan, sits again in a B-25 bomber studying a map of China. To his right is artist Bryan Moon, who, with Hank Potter and four others, made the first expedition to China to search for the remains of the Doolittle bombers.

Master of Ceremonies CHARLIE BOONE from WCCO Radio will first overview the epic first bombing raid on Japan led by legendary "Jimmy" Doolittle. Trained in secret and transported across the Pacific on the aircraft carrier Hornet, sixteen B.25 bombers attacked five Japanese cities on April 18th 1942. The bomber crews escaped across the China Sea, reaching China at night in a storm. Unable to find a friendly airfield and scattered, four aircraft landed on coastal waters. The other bombers crashed into mountains after their crews parachuted from their aircraft. Nothing had been seen of the bombers since the night of April 18th 1942 or of the Chinese people who rescued the crews.

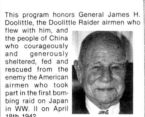

Leader of the 1990 China Expedition to search for five of the lost Doolittle bombers, Frontenac artist/adventurer BRYAN MOON takes the audience into the mountains of Zhejiang Province, unvisited by any foreigners since 1942. The search for five of the bombers sets the stage for the first reunion in 50 years of surviving bomber crew members with the original Chinese people who came to their rescue. With spectacular photographs taken by Expedition photographer Arthur Gibson, THE DOOLITTLE RAID presentation is written, produced and directed by Bryan Moon.

This program honors General James H. Doolittle, the Doolittle Raider airmen who flew with him, and the people of China who courageously and generously sheltered, fed and rescued from the enemy the American airmen who took part in the first bombing raid on Japan in WW. II on April 18th 1942.

This program is further dedicated to the memory of the 1990 Doolittle Raider China Expedition's photographer Arthur Gibson whose photography illustrates THE DOOLITTLE RAID. Arthur suffered a heart attack immediately following the Expedition in September 1990 and died on January 29th 1992 from a subsequent heart attack.

This program was made possible by the support of
NORTHWEST AIRLINES
and with the cooperation of
THE PEOPLE'S ASSOCIATION FOR FRIENDSHIP WITH FOREIGN COUNTRIES, ZHEJIANG PROVINCE, CHINA.

Representing the PAFFC is

Council Member
Mr. HUANG Enbo.

Interpreter
Mr. LI Wen.

The 1990 China

Photo taken at the press conference which ... Expedition. Left to right: Retired Colonel " ... physical fitness instructor, Chinese Consul ... conference (but did not join the Expedition), a ... Vice President of the Hadley Companies who ... tor Tom Wier, retired Brigadier General from ... Expedition's doctor.

THE DOOLITTLE RAID and 50th Anniversary Reunio...

No. 1 Bomber. The Search and reunion.		No. 11 Bomber. The Search and Reunion.	No. 3 Bomber. The Search and Reunion.	

Co-pilot. Lt. Col. Richard E. Cole.	Navigator. Col. Henry A. Potter.	Navigator. Lt. Col. Frank A. Kappeler.	Navigator. Cpt. Charles J. Ozuk Jr.	Co-p... Col. ...

Present, on stage, will be two of the three surviving members of the lead bomber which was captained by Lt. Col. James H. Doolittle. Audio tape of 95 year old retired General Doolittle will focus on key events prior, during and after the raid. Col. Potter was a member of the 1990 Doolittle Raiders China Expedition. He therefore, will be meeting Mr. Zhu, who saved his life in 1942, for the second time in 50 years.

After corresponding for several years with the man who drove him to safety in his Postal truck, they will be meeting for the first time in 50 years.

Health reasons may prevent Cpt. Ozuk from atte... be represented by his daughter Georgione Ozuk... since 1942 with Mr. Liu who sheltered, fed and gu... of No. 3 bo... Cpl. Leland... bomber No... craft crash... represented... Faktor.

From Shanghai, China
Mr. ZHU Xuesan.
Schoolteacher.

From Jiaxing, China.
Mr. ZENG Jianpei.
Postal Inspector.

From Liu Jai, China
Mr. LIU Fangchiao.
Farmer.

Publicity leaflets produced to mark the 50th anniversary of the Doolittle Raid in 1992.

1992 年"杜利特尔行动"50 周年庆典活动的宣传折页

The Sheldon
Performing Arts Theatre, Est. 1904

iting the grandeur of the past with the excite-
ent of a lively and varied arts program today.

to a faithful restoration in 1988, our turn-of-the-century
atre is filled with the elegance of the past once again. Gild-
plaster reflects the glow of light from brass chandeliers and
catley painted ornament graces our warm, intimate hall
 member of the League of Historic Theatres, the Sheldon was
cribed as a "jewel box" in 1904 and, now after our locally
ded $3.5 million restoration, can once again be described
Red Wing's "jewel box" theatre.

h year the Sheldon presents the widest variety and the
est quality in entertainment and the performing arts. Local,
onal and international artists are represented in our
ented and locally produced programs, community outreach
ices and residencies with local and regional schools.

invite you to place your name on our mailing list to keep
ent with the wonderful programs presented at the Sheldon.
Box 34, Red Wing, Minnesota, #612-388-2806.

A copy of the original Reunion Program (1992)

The Sheldon
Performing Arts Theatre, Est. 1904
RED WING, MINNESOTA
March 22nd 1992.

Commemorative Program

The 50th
Anniversary and first reunion of
Doolittle Raider crew survivors
with the original Chinese people
who came to their rescue on
April 18th 1942.

In the Bryan Moon Production of

THE DOOLITTLE RAID

dition members

d preceded the
Heidi Olson, a
ened the press
n, Joyce Olson,
's art, and Doc-
Reserve and the

Arthur Gibson, the Ex-
pedition's photograph-
er. Ex RAF and fellow of
the British Royal Photo-
graphic Society.

No. 7 Bomber.
The Search and Reunion.

No. 15 Bomber.
The Search and Reunion.

nport.

Navigator.
Cpt. Charles L. McClure.

Engineer/Gunner.
Sgt. David J. Thatcher.

Co-pilot.
Maj. Griffith Williams.

Engineer/Gunner.
Lt. Col. Edward Saylor.

ase he will
st meeting
members

gunner of
en the air-
e will be
Mr. Bud

No. 7 bomber was captained by Lt. Ted Lawson who wrote the book "30
Seconds Over Tokyo". Lt. Lawson died just two months before this first 50th
reunion of his three surviving crew members with the Chinese doctor who
helped to save their lives after the
crash landing of their aircraft on
the coast of China in 1942.

Two of the four surviving members
of this crew will meet, for the first
time in 50 years, the Chinese lady
who fed and sheltered them after
their bomber landed off the coast
of China in 1942.

From Linhai, China
Dr. CHEN Shenyan.

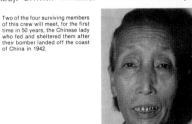

From Tan Toushan Island, China
Mrs. ZHAO Xiaobao.
Fisherman's wife.

The US Air Force Academy issuing a certificate
to Liu Fangqiao to honor his contribution.
美国空军学院为刘芳桥颁发奖状

Zhao Xiaobao with US crewmen she rescued.
赵小宝和被救飞行员合影

Col. Henry A. Potter,
Xuesan again.
朱学三与被救的美国

ican pilot, meeting Zhu

特在一起

Zeng Jianpei with US crewmen he rescued.
曾健培与被救飞行员合影

Chen Shenyan with US crewmen he rescued.
陈慎言与被救飞行员合影

When the US inspection group visited China to search for wreckage of the crashed bombers in 1994, the group members posed for a picture in front of the Enze Medical Bureau where some wounded Americans received medical treatment.

1994年美国考察团来华寻访，在当年医治受伤飞行员的恩泽医局前合影

Col. Henry A. Potter shaking hands with Wang Xiaofu in Xiangshan.

飞行员波特与象山渔民王小富握手

Letters exchanged between Zeng Jianpei and some US crewmen he rescued.
曾健培和美国飞行员的书信来往

September 12, 1989

Jian-pei Zeng
No. 5104 5th Building
Ye-Jin Alley No. 2
Jiaxing 314000
Zhejiang Province
China

Dear Jian-pei Zeng,

Thank you for your thoughtful letter of July 24th just received. Thanks also for your "hospitality" to the "Hari Karier" crew. The two men you spoke of are deceased. Capt. Greening passed away in 1957 and Lt. Reddy died, during the war, in 1942. The other 3 members of the crew were:

Col. Frank A. Kappeler (Navigator)
1527 Riebli Road
Santa Rosa, CA95404

William L. Birch (Bombardier)   Sgt. Gardner (Engineer-Gunner)
2126 W. Elder   Killed in action June, 1942
Santa Ana, CA 92704

A belated thank you for your efforts. Many of us owe our lives to the bravery of the Chinese people during April of 1942.

Every good wish for much happiness and good health. May the people of China achieve their goals.

Very sincerely,

Place where Lt. Col. Doolittle landed in his parachute: Group members and villagers recalling what happened.
杜利特尔中校跳伞处,考察团和村民回忆着当年的情景。

Col. Henry A. Potter giving a warm hug to Zhu Xushan.
飞行员波特与朱学三拥抱

March 26, 1946

My very good friend, Sho San,

It was with very great pleasure that I received your letter of December 17, 1945. Since that day in April 1942 when first we met, my thoughts of you have been many. Many times I have wondered whether or not you came safely through the war, so you can easily understand my feelings when your most welcome letter came.

I am sure that had it not been for your timely assistance, myself and Sgt Fred Braemer, who was with me when we met, and S/Sgt Paul Leonard, whom in searching for we climbed many mountains, would have had a much more difficult experience.

After leaving the kind hospitality of you and your friends, we journeyed to Chungking, where we had the honor to be introduced to the great leaders of your country. From there many of us returned to the United States for a short period of time. After that myself and other members of the group which first bombed Japan were sent to North Africa where we fought the Germans and Italians. During this period our friend, Paul Leonard, was killed. During a German air raid a bomb fell into his shelter destroying him and others. We all felt sad over this.

On the very day that you wrote to me, all of the group, who was still alive, had a reunion in the state of Florida. Past experiences were told and retold. Among those told was how you helped us out of our difficulties. Fred Braemer and I wondered then and still wish to know the answer to the following questions. Please answer if you remember. On that morning when you met us on the road, did you know that we were Americans? Had you been sent for to come and help us? We were worried not knowing whether or not we were among friends.

I often think back to my first morning in China and the first village I was in. There was a most dignified gentlemen who came out with his brush and ink, thinking to communicate with me by writing. I, of course, could not understand his writing and he could not understand mine. His name I do not know. If ever you are in that village and if you know the name of that gentleman, it is my desire that you thank him for his attempt to aid me. Many of the other villagers were most kind and desirous of helping also.

The first breakfast we had together is also a fond memory to me. Many people were there. Everything was excellent. I remember that someone asked if I were married. I was not then married but may be married a short time from now.

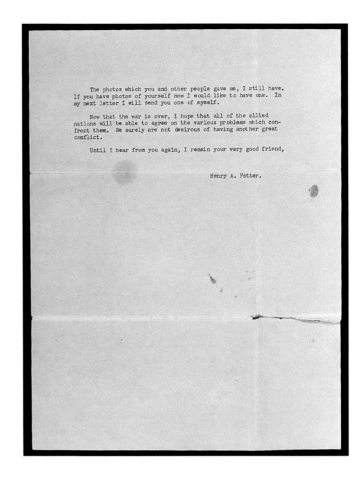

The photos which you and other people gave me, I still have. If you have photos of yourself now I would like to have one. In my next letter I will send you one of myself.

Now that the war is over, I hope that all of the allied nations will be able to agree on the various problems which confront them. We surely are not desirous of having another great conflict.

Until I hear from you again, I remain your very good friend,

Henry A. Potter.

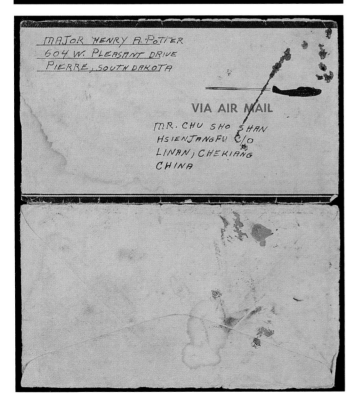

MAJOR HENRY A. POTTER
604 W. PLEASANT DRIVE
PIERRE, SOUTH DAKOTA

VIA AIR MAIL

MR. CHU SHO SHAN
HSIEN JANG FU C/O
LINAN, CHEKIANG
CHINA

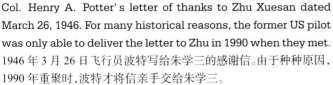

Col. Henry A. Potter's letter of thanks to Zhu Xuesan dated March 26, 1946. For many historical reasons, the former US pilot was only able to deliver the letter to Zhu in 1990 when they met.
1946 年 3 月 26 日飞行员波特写给朱学三的感谢信。由于种种原因，1990 年重聚时，波特才将信亲手交给朱学三。

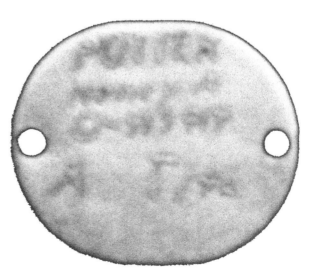

Col. Henry A. Potter, a US pilot, presented a wrist badge to Zhu Xuesan when he was rescued.
飞行员波特被救后赠给朱学三的腕章

Plates of thanks signed by 44 rescued US crewmen presented by the US inspection group to the Chinese rescuers.

1990 年考察团赠给中国营救人员的"多谢牌",上面有 44 名被救飞行员的签名。

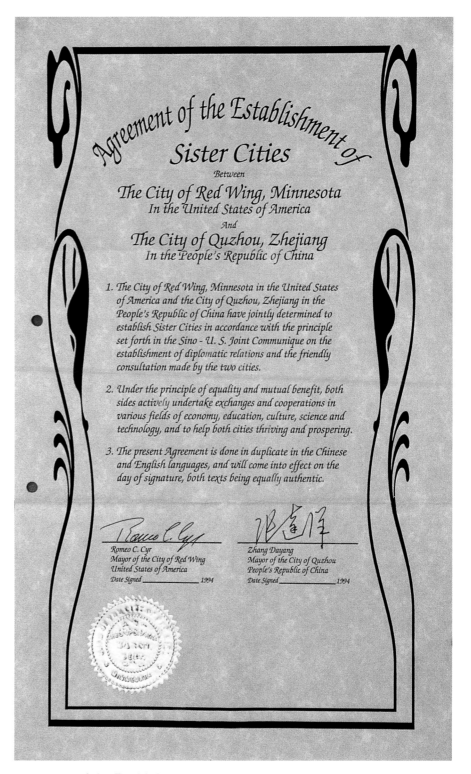

Agreement of the Establishment of Sister Cities Between the City of Red Wing, Minnesota in the USA and the City of Quzhou, Zhejiang in the PRC.

衢州市与雷德温市结为友好城市协议书

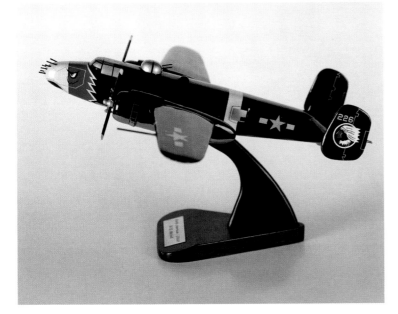

The model of B-25 bomber presented to the People's Government of Quzhou City by the City of Red Wing in 1997.

1997 年雷德温市赠给衢州市人民政府的 B-25 型轰炸机模型。

Presented to

Zeng Jianpei

with heartfelt gratitude
from the men and women
of the
United States Air Force Academy

感 谢

Plates of thanks from US Air Force Academy when five Chinese
senior citizens visited the United States in 1992.
1992 年 5 位中国老人访美，美国空军学院赠送的"感谢牌"。

Medals of honor presented to the Chinese.
赠给中国老人的奖章

Paper clippings Zhu Xuesan collected.
朱学三收藏的剪报

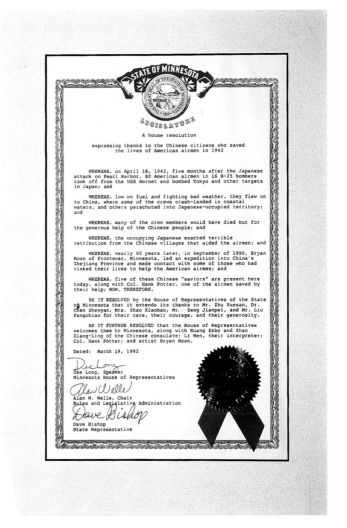

Letter of thanks.
感谢信

Porcelain jar presented to Zhao Xiaobao.
赠给赵小宝的瓷罐

A part of pictures in this pictorial is equated from *China Airlift—The Hump* written by the China-Burma-India Hump Pilots Association. Thanks a lot the support of the China-Burma-India Hump Pilots Association to our publication of the pictorial.

该书部分图片选自中缅印驼峰飞行员协会出版的《中国空运——驼峰》一书,感谢中缅印驼峰飞行员协会对该书出版的支持。

（以姓氏笔划为序）

编　　委：干　飞　马登潮　戈叔亚　邓美瑛　龙建民　吴中培　张长虹　张礼毅
　　　　　张宝贵　汤汉清　杨安兴　周云祥　周保昌　赵　金　赵东平　段汇成
　　　　　胡晓阳　胡德盛　徐康明　晏友琼　黄明辉　韩李敏　葛洪保
撰　　稿：龙建民　吴中培　陈立三　赵东平　杨安兴　胡晓阳　傅　康　葛洪保
编　　务：李　军　张琼丽　曹建明　鲍珍玲

史学顾问：耿成宽　周小宁
英文翻译：王国振　夏文义　高翠灵　施明辉
英文审校：王国振
责任编辑：汤贺伟
装帧设计：闫志杰
插　　图：龙力游　孙　逊　程可槑

图书在版编目（CIP）数据
历史的记忆：英汉对照/云南省人民政府新闻办公室等编.
——北京：五洲传播出版社，2002.10
ISBN 7-5085-0121-7
Ⅰ．历…　Ⅱ．云…　Ⅲ．①抗日战争（1937-1945）—中美关系—史料—图集 ② 中美关系—友好往来—
史料—图集　Ⅳ. K265.06-64
中国版本图书馆 CIP 数据核字（2002）第 073660 号

The Memory of History
历史的记忆

五洲传播出版社
地址：中国北京北三环中路 31 号　邮编：100088　电话：(86) 10 82008174，82008228
网址：www.cicc.org.cn

开本：230mm*295mm　1/16　印张：10.5
2002 年 10 月第一版　第一次印刷　印数：1-7000 册
ISBN 7-5085-0121-7/K·367
定价：260.00 元